The Cable Car Book

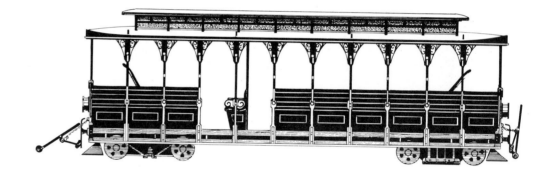

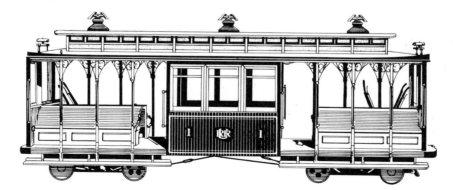

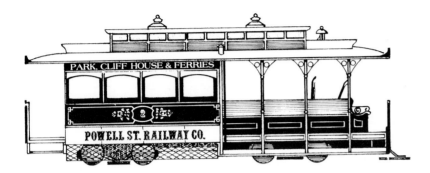

Charles Smallwood
Warren Edward Miller
Don DeNevi

THE CABLE CAR BOOK

BONANZA BOOKS
New York

This 1983 edition is published by Bonanza Books, distributed by Crown Publishers, Inc., by arrangement with Celestial Arts.

Cover design by Linda Herman
Book design by Abigail Johnston
Drawings on title page by Lester Krames
Photograph on back cover by Stephen W. Fotter.
Diagrams on pages 19, 21, and 22 are used with the permission of San Francisco Cable Car Museum/Pacific Coast Chapter, Railway & Locomotive History Society, Inc.

Permission to reproduce the comic strip *Travels with Farley* by Phil Frank has been granted by the artist and Chronicle Features, San Francisco.

Manufactured in the United States of America

Library of Congress Cataloging in Publication Data

Smallwood, Charles A., 1912–
    The cable car book.

    Bibliography: p.
    Includes index.
    1. Railroads, Cable—United States—History.
I. Miller, Warren, 1924–   II. DeNevi, Don, 1937–
III. Title.
[TF835.S53 1983]   625'.5   82-24472
ISBN: 0-517-408783

h g f e d c b a

A Note About the Photographs

This book owes its existence to the unknown photographers of San Francisco's youth. Many of the photographs gathered here are by amateurs—early practitioners of a developing art—who tramped the hills and cobbled streets burdened with cumbersome equipment and possessed of great patience. Photography in those days was a long way from instamatic.

We are also grateful to the private collectors who preserved these early photographs in scrapbooks and attics so that we may enjoy them, and learn from them, today and through the years to come.

As both the art of picture taking and the city of San Francisco matured, amateur photographers became professional, and their names became known. Museums, libraries, and archives were founded, and the images of our past were assured protection.

In selecting the photographs for this book, we endeavored to choose prints made from the original glass plates or negatives. Failing that, we tried to find the earliest known print. Many of these original plates, negatives, and prints were contributed by Charles Smallwood, and unless otherwise credited, the photographs in this book are from his extensive collection.

We would like to thank the following people, libraries and collections—past and present—who have directly and indirectly made this book possible: F. Bagnasio; The Bancroft Library, University of California, Berkeley; Peter Breing; Randolph Brandt; Chaney Collection; Joe Chapman; Christian Brothers Provincial Archives; Harre Demoro; Victor DuBrutz; Phil Fein; Otis Fleming Collection; Goldsmith Brothers; Roy Graves; Tom Gray; Robert M. Hanft; Grahame Hardy; T. E. Hecht; Holler; Fred Mathews; C.D. Miller; Warren K. Miller; Muhlmann Collection; Oakland Public Library; San Francisco Cable Car Museum; San Francisco Public Library; Richard Schlaich; Walt Sievers; Silliman Brothers; Stanford University Archives; Louis Stein; Clarence J. Sweet; Tabor; U.S. Maritime Museum; Bert Ward; Watkins, and Wilbur C. Whitaker.

The Authors

CONTENTS

The Cable Car Book

PROLOGUE

In 1776, Lieutenant Joaquin Moraga, second in command to Colonel Juan Bautista de Anza of the expeditionary forces sent to Alta California by the Spanish Viceroy in Mexico City, established a military post at the Presidio beside the Golden Gate and selected the site for Father Junipero Serra's Mission of San Francisco de Asis—Mission Dolores. Seven years earlier, Don Gaspar de Portola, on an unsuccessful excursion to locate Monterey Bay, sighted San Francisco Bay instead, and noted in his diary that he had "found nothing."

Thus, while thousands of miles to the east a band of discontents was fighting to create what was to become the United States of America, white men first settled on the wind- and fog-swept sand dunes of Yerba Buena

The little town of San Francisco before the discovery of gold. Montgomery Street bordered the shoreline in those days. With the coming of the Forty-niners, and the need for more level land near the trading center at the harbor, San Franciscans extended their city into Yerba Buena Cove using sand, dirt, garbage, and spoiled merchandise as landfill. (The Bancroft Library.)

Cove. The tiny settlement of tents was still chiefly a sailor's port of call when, in 1835, an Englishman named Richardson founded the town of Yerba Buena as distinct from the mission and military outposts. On July 4, 1836, the town celebrated the completion of its first permanent structure, a two-story frame trading post built by American Jacob P. Leese. Ten years later, there were perhaps 50 buildings clustered around Portsmouth Square and 200 inhabitants. But the town was still far from prepossessing and its streets were nothing more than dirt tracks that became swampy ditches during the rainy season.

On January 30, 1847, Washington A. Bartlett, who had been appointed *alcalde* (mayor) of Yerba Buena following President Polk's declaration of

This 1850 view of the burgeoning city and crowded harbor was taken by W. Shew from a vantage point in Portsmouth Square. Landfill operations had not yet begun. Rincon Hill, which was leveled in later years, is at far right. (The Bancroft Library.)

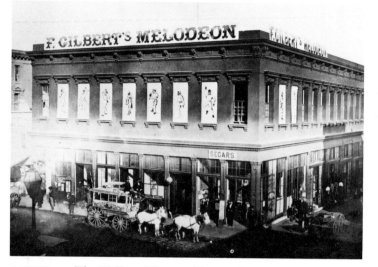

ABOVE: *The Yellow Line at Clay and Kearny Streets. (The Bancroft Library.)*

RIGHT.   *The first street railway. A steam dummy double-decked car at Market and Third Streets.*

war on Mexico, issued a decree officially changing the name of the town to San Francisco. A year later, gold was discovered by James Marshall in the tailrace of Johann August Sutter's mill on the south fork of the American River, 120 miles to the northeast. Almost overnight, San Francisco was transformed. In 1850, California became a state and San Francisco had a population of over twenty thousand.

The town had become a pulsing hub of merchants and entrepreneurs. To get the goods and people through, adequate streets, as well as public transportation, were needed. Most of the streets were laid out on the flatlands along the Bay and along the lines of least resistance which ran southward. The many steep hills—some rising to a height of 900 feet—were believed to be major obstacles in expanding westward, and the slow growth of the city in that direction justified that belief. A few hardy souls settled on the hills that rose up behind the bustling centers of commerce, but most found their horses unwilling to tackle the grades.

In 1852 the first public omnibus line began operation. For the staggering fee of fifty cents on weekdays and a dollar on Sundays, the horse-drawn "Yellow Line" carried passengers along streets and roads that ran from the Post Office at Clay and Kearny Streets to Mission Dolores. Soon there were many other lines, their routes crisscrossing all of downtown San Francisco, and the fares were reduced to ten cents.

On July 4, 1860, The San Francisco Market Street Railroad Company made a bid to replace the horse, when it began operating the city's first steam-powered street railway, employing a locomotive masked by a "dummy" car that was intended not to terrify the many horses plying its route out Market and Valencia Streets to Seventeenth Street. Though this installation did not precipitate a rush towards replacing the horse, by the early 1870s, it was obvious that new transportation methods were indeed needed to handle not only congestion in the core of the city but to open the way for building on the nearby hills and westward. While many owners and real estate speculators insisted that the prestige and charm of South Park, Rincon Hill, and the Mission area "warm belt" would outweigh any attractions offered by foggier and chillier parts of the city, it was clear that people of wealth, and the less affluent as well, had their sights on the commanding hills. The time had come for the cable car.

THE ENDLESS ROPEWAY

Andrew Smith was born in England in 1836, two years before W. J. Curtis—an Englishman with American tramway experience—had patented a gripping mechanism which could quickly grasp and release a moving cable, and one year after his father, a Scot, had taken out the first patent in Great Britain for the manufacture of wire rope. Andrew, who later adapted the surname of his uncle and godfather, Sir Andrew Hallidie, a physician to Queen Victoria, came to California in 1882. He mined the gold fields, and at the tender age of nineteen he designed and built a 200-foot wire suspension bridge across the middle fork of the American River near Sacramento. Soon young Hallidie, following in his father's footsteps, constructed a wire rope making machine, the product of which was used to pull ore-filled cars up a track from the mines. He moved his wire rope manufacturing plant to San Francisco, where he and his associates designed and constructed suspension bridges and one of the several types of aerial tramways used by mine operators in California and throughout the Far West. The prelude to his cable car planning was his patent for what he called an "endless ropeway," and the securing of a street railroad franchise from Benjamin Brooks, who also had a dream of an endless ropeway but not the money to construct it.

Andrew Smith Hallidie.
(University of California Archives.)

On a wet, drizzly day in 1869, a civil and mechanical engineer of San Francisco stood on the corner of Stockton and Jackson Streets, conversing with a friend. A street car of the Omnibus line, which then climbed the somewhat steep grade from Dupont to Stockton on Jackson Street, was seen approaching, drawn by five horses. One of the horses slipped, a vain effort was made to raise him, and a mild panic ensued as the heavily laden car slid back to Dupont Street, dragging the prostrate horse. Both gentlemen looked on with concern. The one, the senior member of a well-known lithographic firm, said, half impatiently to the other, "Andrew, why don't you go to work and invent something to pull streetcars safely up steep grades and prevent such accidents?"

His companion replied thoughtfully that he had been studying on something of the sort for a year past. He concluded to renew his experiments. In 1870 he obtained a patent on a grip pulley made for transmitting power from the engine to a rope to prevent slipping. The principles he had already firmly fixed in his mind, for he had placed something of the kind in operation in the mines for the transportation of ores, but the application of the same principle to a railway on the public streets of a city

presented many obstacles and difficulties. It was necessary to have a railway so arranged as to afford no obstruction to ordinary travel. The cars must be capable of being stopped at any point. The grades would be varying, and the rope must be so arranged that it could be kept down and not fly up unexpectedly in the air. The difficulties were finally overcome, and in 1871 the inventor, Andrew S. Hallidie, induced Joseph Britton, Henry L. Davis and James Moffitt to join him in his undertaking to put his invention in practical order. In order to secure certain necessary privileges they had discreetly kept their names secret, but one day it was divulged in confidence to the editor of a Sacramento paper, who forwarded the information by telegraph to his paper, in which it appeared the following day. It was probably due to this untimely publication that a swiftly organized company succeeded, in advance of them, in procuring the right to run up Russian Hill an indefinite sort of permit with a winding route, but which sufficed to check the progress of the wire rope railway company.

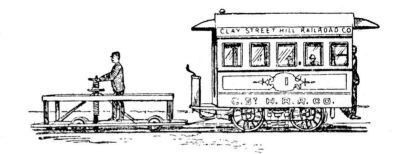

Early sketch of the first passenger-carrying cable car used in the United States.

They went speedily to work and completed a track along Clay Street, from Kearny to Jones. A working model of the system had long been exhibited in the office of the attorney of the company, but it was not viewed with much confidence or respect by the visiting public. It was a neat little model, with well-laid track representing all the grades, the cable in operation and dummies sliding up and down, but everybody ridiculed and laughed at it.

At last the principle of the model was to be practically tried. About 3 o'clock on the morning of the 1st of August, 1873, while nearly all of the city was sleeping, a little party of eager, excited men gathered at the brow of Clay Street hill where the street plunges down the steep incline from Jones to Kearny. The descent is 307 feet, and the distance about 3000 feet. From Jones to Taylor is the steepest plane, the grade being one foot to every 6.15 feet. The inventor was calm and confident, but his friends extremely timorous and skeptical. The dummy, a mere skeleton affair, with four wheels of about equal size, was fitted with a semi-circular strap-brake over the tops of the wheels. Safety straps were attached (being tied around a telegraph pole), and the concern was lowered down a little distance and then brought back. Besides the brakes mentioned, long pieces of scantling were attached to the wheels, improvised as additional checks on any undue velocity which the car might assume on its downward progress.

An old locomotive engineer named Hewitt had been engaged to run the dummy, but when he looked down the terrible descent into the gulf of darkness below he turned pale, trembled, and said to Mr. Hallidie: "I think perhaps you had better take this down, boss."

The inventor took his place at the helm, while his friends, in great trepidation lest the thing should "get away and kill somebody," took charge of the wheels, and to the surprise of the majority made the round trip in safety. On the afternoon of the same day the first trip with a car attached was essayed. The crowd along the track was so large that it was with great difficulty anything could be done. Although none of the anticipated terrors were realized, people were timid about trusting themselves on the cars; and it is a laughable recollection now that in order to gain patronage of the road it was found necessary to give the public free rides for two days, while for some time it was impossible to run the cars after dark.*

At the time, Hallidie commented, "The operation was an earnest one. There was no frivolity. The whole affair was serious, and when it was done there was simply a mutual hand shaking and nothing but cold water drunk. I do not know whether I felt more rejoiced at the visible proofs of the success of the trial trip, than at the expression of satisfaction, relief and renewed confidence in the faces of the gentlemen who had invested the money and faith in the enterprise, and had stood by it so faithfully."

Cable haulage was nothing new in itself. But this, its successful application to public street transport, was indeed new. Hallidie's cable road was a simple affair, only seven blocks long, but the promise offered by the pioneering line in Clay Street hit the world of transportation engineering like a bomb. It demonstrated the feasibility of surmounting the hills by such a mode of traction, afforded the actual means to settle neglected parts of the city, and provided an answer to many frustrating problems of locomotion and rails in city streets. Although it was an instant success, it remained to be seen whether the cable car would prove practical in more diverse situations than Clay Street. The great cost of installation dampened the enthusiastic curiosity of many others, and it was more than three years before a second cable line was opened in San Francisco.

Henry Casebolt, owner of the Sutter Street Railway and proprietor of a large machine works, converted his horsecar line to cable in 1877 and his company's stock appreciated markedly while his operating costs fell. Casebolt was already well-known for his astonishing "balloon" horsecar which ran along Market Street. The carriage was on a pivot above the wheelbase. At the end of the line, the carriage and the horses were turned in a half-circle, and the direction of the car reversed without turning its wheels.

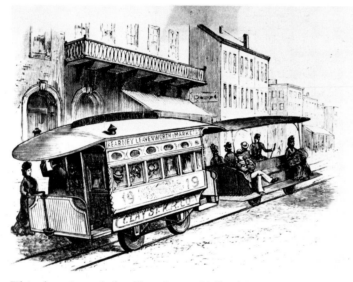

This drawing of the Clay Street Hill cable train appeared in Harper's Weekly in the 1870s. By the time Hallidie's new road opened for revenue service, a month after the pre-dawn trial run, seats for passengers had been installed on the grip car.

*San Francisco Chronicle, 1887.

Passersby often stopped and helped to turn the carriage, establishing a precedent for the activity at cable car turntables of today. Also, in the hope of overcoming some of the maintenance problems created by a system the arteries of which lay underground, Casebolt conceived the plan of placing the cables overhead. The result was an odd-looking model which actually ran for four months across the bay in the Piedmont hills. On the roof of the car was an elaborate, Art Nouveau device that grasped at cables that ran through brackets supported at roof level on lamp posts. The idea was not unlike the idea behind modern-day electric streetcars, but at the time all those posts, poles and overhead wires were deemed unsightly, and Casebolt could get no backing for his plan. He went on to design improvements in the grip mechanism as used by Hallidie, and to utilize the refinements in his own system.

Casebolt wasn't the only one to alter, improve, and adjust the mechanics of cable car traction. In fact, a number of men—notably William E. Eppelsheimer, who had been Hallidie's draftsman, Asa E. Hovey, a foreman in Casebolt's machine works, and Henry Root—played considerably larger roles in the development of the cable car, in San Francisco as well as elsewhere, than did Hallidie himself.

Casebolt's "balloon" cars were lavish in their interior appointments, having such niceties as plush upholstered seats and carpeted floors. They were said to be great favorites of the ladies, and two of them lived out their retirement years as genteel, stationary tea rooms.

A California Street cable train passing the mansion of the line's chief promoter, Leland Stanford. At the top of the hill is the extravaganza of Mark Hopkins. 1883. (The Bancroft Library.)

The third cable car line, which began operation in 1878, was the California Street Cable Railroad. Promoted by Leland Stanford and designed by Henry Root, it, like the Clay Street Hill line, attacked the steep grade of Nob Hill, which had been named for the gold- and silver-rich "nabobs" who continued their rivalry by building one mansion more extraordinary than the last on its summit and slopes.

In the 1880s other cities in the country incorporated cable car traction into their transportation systems. Successful systems were built and operated in a number of cities, including Chicago, Philadelphia, Kansas City, Cincinnati, New York, Los Angeles, St. Louis, Seattle, Denver, Spokane, Washington, D.C., and Portland, Oregon. And in 1886 the city of Oakland across the bay saw the opening of the first of its own two cable lines. In all, 28 United States cities succumbed to the appeal of the cable car; a number of others had begun construction of cable car lines; and there were foreign installations in New Zealand, Australia, Great Britain, Paris, and Lisbon, before the cable car ceased to be economical.

Oakland Cable Railway.
(Louis Stein Collection.)

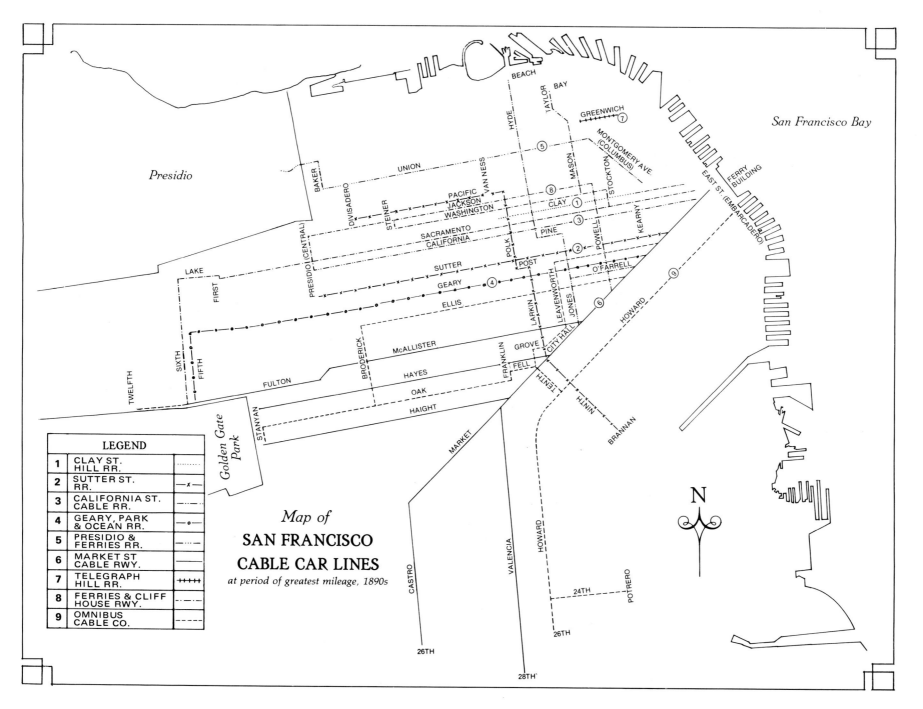

Map of
SAN FRANCISCO
CABLE CAR LINES
at period of greatest mileage, 1890s

LEGEND		
1	CLAY ST. HILL RR.	....
2	SUTTER ST. RR.	—x—
3	CALIFORNIA ST. CABLE RR.	—·—
4	GEARY, PARK & OCEAN RR.	—o—
5	PRESIDIO & FERRIES RR.	———
6	MARKET ST CABLE RWY.	———
7	TELEGRAPH HILL RR.	+++++
8	FERRIES & CLIFF HOUSE RWY.	—··—
9	OMNIBUS CABLE CO.	- - - -

San Francisco Bay

Presidio

Golden Gate Park

N

The era of the cable car in San Francisco reached its peak in the early 1890s. At that time there were eight different companies and some twenty lines. There were more than 25 miles of track. Two hundred and eight cable cars made a total of 2,048 round trips daily at seven to twelve miles an hour. And while many variations of the grip mechanism had been designed, patented and put into use, some mechanical engineers criticized the efforts. Bucknall Smith, a leading English engineer, wrote: "Although all such cable tramways are founded on the same general principle, yet no two lines appear to be constructed exactly alike, and the modifications adopted in many cases do not seem to be the result of experience. This lack of similarity may in fact be attributed to the patent mania which has beset the development of the system, and to the different interests fostered by the various engineers and others who were the patentees."*

The quibbles of outsiders notwithstanding, San Franciscans were well pleased by the cables. The system operated with such a degree of safety as to inspire public confidence. None of the passengers seemed fearful while riding the steep grades. But they were, perhaps, accustomed to rowdy travel. An old story has it that an early horsecar on a cobbled grade jumped the track, broke loose from its horses, and rolled all the way to the foot of the hill over the cobblestones without the passengers being aware of anything unusual. Cable companies repaved many streets at their own expense, replacing the dirt and cobbles that made horse and horsecar traction possible, first with planking, and then, increasingly, more substantial pavings of rock blocks supported upon cement. From the very first, the companies tried to please their passengers with excellent service. The cars were not only timed for transfer connections with other lines (at midday the waiting time between cars was from two to seven minutes), but they were scrupulously cleaned every night. Neatly uniformed employees were polite and attentive and the only suggestion for improvement passengers had was greater speed on the city's outlying lines.

*J. Bucknall Smith, *A Treatise Upon Cable Or Rope Traction*, p. 40.

HOW IT WORKS

The basic concept of cable traction was simple: An endless cable is kept in motion throughout the route. The car is equipped with a vise-like grip that catches the moving wire rope when the operator desires the car to move forward and disengages the rope when he wants to stop. The actual deployment of the cable, the supplying of power to move the cable, and the grip mechanism, however, were far from simple, presenting many problems for the engineers to overcome.

The cable is housed beneath the streets, kept at a relatively constant depth by an intricate system of pulleys, bars, and sheaves. The cable tunnel is some two feet deep and 18 inches wide, and was constructed with cast iron units and lined with metal and wood. The wire rope is carried through the tunnel on pulleys; the cable is moved by winding wheels ten feet in diameter, turned, in the early days, by a steam engine located in a powerhouse at either end of the line, or at a convenient point between. The speed with which the car moved was determined by the speed of the cable, which was regulated by the revolutions of the driving wheel at the powerhouse.

If it pleases Providence to make a car run up and down a slit in the ground for many miles, and if for two-pence I can ride in that car, why shall I seek the reasons of the miracle?

RUDYARD KIPLING

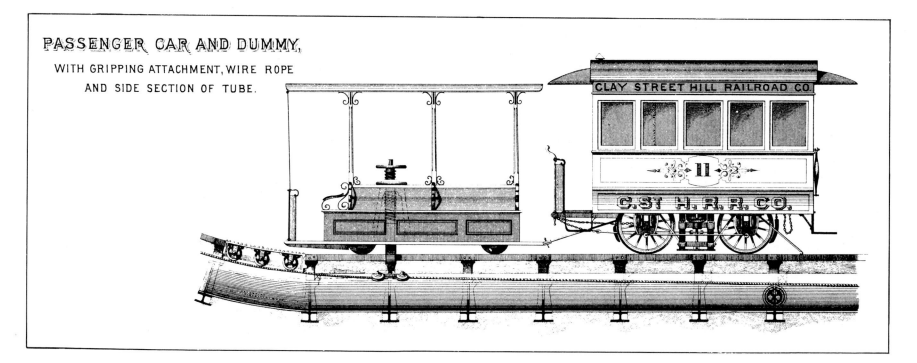

PASSENGER CAR AND DUMMY,

WITH GRIPPING ATTACHMENT, WIRE ROPE
AND SIDE SECTION OF TUBE.

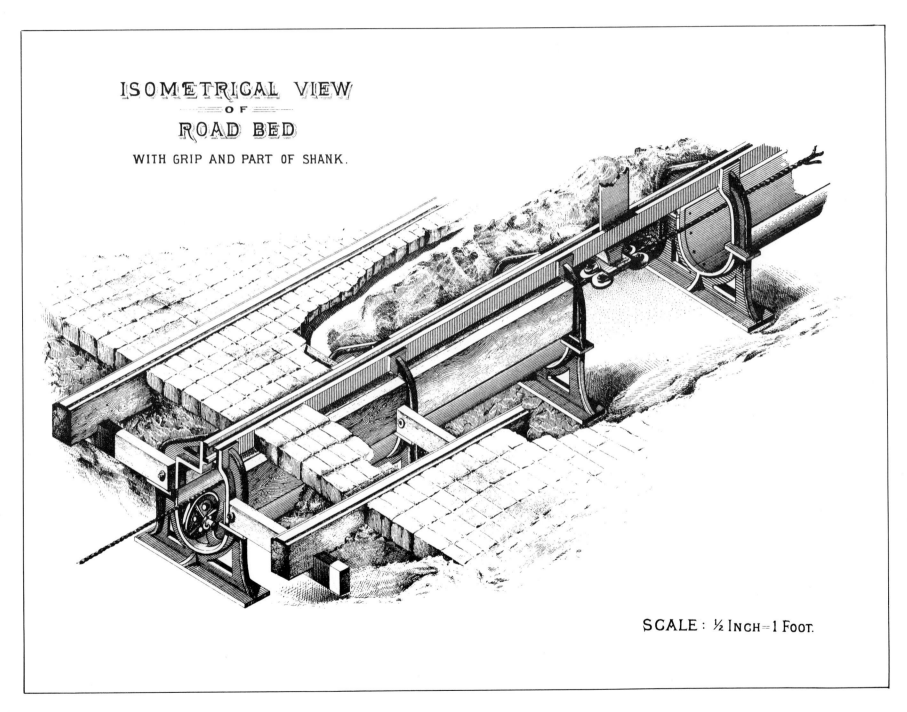

ISOMETRICAL VIEW
OF
ROAD BED

WITH GRIP AND PART OF SHANK.

SCALE : ½ INCH = 1 FOOT.

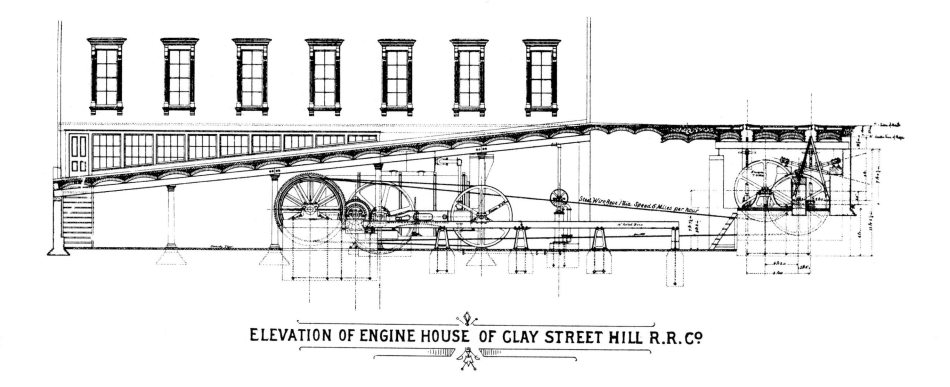

ELEVATION OF ENGINE HOUSE OF CLAY STREET HILL R.R. Co.

The first powerhouse was located at the corner of Clay and Leavenworth Streets at the top of the hill. It was a plain wooden building, 68 x 68 feet, consisting of two stories and a basement. From that simple little structure, the original Clay Street line was run between August 1873 and 1891. In the winding room of the small power station were two 150-horsepower engines coupled to the same shaft, although only one at a time was operated. The power was transmitted from the engine shaft to the rope winding drum. As the cable entered the winding room, it would pass around the winding wheels, under a tension wheel, and issue out again into the street to proceed along the line. The local slack in a cable, fluctuating according to the loads on the individual cars and also according to the amount of starting and stopping along the route, was taken up by the tension wheel. Moving up and down with the increase or decrease in the slack, the weight of the wheel bearing down on the cable would maintain a constant tension, thus preventing any undue jerking of the line.

UPPER RIGHT.   *Inside the Washington and Mason Street car barn, 1900.*

LOWER RIGHT.   *Inside the Washington and Mason Street powerhouse today. The basic technology has not changed much, though now electricity drives engines of much greater horsepower than was available to Hallidie. (Curt W. Kaldor, courtesy The Cable Car Museum.)*

TOP.   *Cable splicers (known as ropemen). This method of splicing cable has not changed for over a century.*

BOTTOM.   *Building a cable road at Market and Hayes Streets. (Louis Stein Collection.)*

Another kind of slack occurs due to the tendency of a cable, especially a new one, to stretch after it is put into use. Steel "take-up" cleats make it possible for the winding wheels to be moved back to compensate for the stretch and keep the tension constant. They also make it possible to move the wheel up, so that when a cable is broken and needs to be spliced, the line can be loosened until the damage is repaired.

At the base of hills and at low points on relatively level ground along the line, it is necessary to use small pulleys set in a movable beam underground to keep the cable down in the slot, away from the tunnel roof. These depression pulleys are also used to carry the cable below an intersecting line. Pulleys carrying the wire rope under the streets are placed some 50 feet apart, with depression beams and pulleys located where needed. On curves, the cable rests on a series of closely set pulleys on the inside of the arc, while the grip pulls the cable away from the axis as it negotiates the turn.

The original track was laid with a 30 pound T-rail with a 3-foot 6-inch gauge. The slot was placed to the side of the center of the track so that the rope would not work directly beneath it. Over 7,000 feet in length, 15/16" in diameter, the original rope was first operated at a speed of four miles an hour. The total rise in the first line's distance of 2,791 feet was 307 feet, grades being as steep as 17 percent.

Hallidie's prototype grip was operated by a wheel-driven rack and pinion. This gripping attachment, connected with the car and passing through the narrow slot in the tunnel, transmitted the motion of the cable to the car. The cable was grasped by a grip fed through pulleys. The pulleys pressed against the moving cable first, then the steel dies of the grip, and this allowed the car to start up smoothly. The rack-and-pinion grip was never used, however, and a similar screw-within-a-screw mechanism was developed before Hallidie's first car was put into operation.

The grip used on the original car was operated by means of two hand wheels, a large hollow screw and a threaded rod which passed through it. By using a hollow screw, the grip could be raised or lowered to pick up or release the rope. The jaws of the grip, which were supported by an L-shaped foot carrying two sliding frames, were operated by an upper hand wheel and threaded rod. The main grip dies were supplemented at each end by a pair of horizontal grooved wheels designed to pick up the rope and hold it in position between the jaws. The jaws and wheels were closed on the rope by

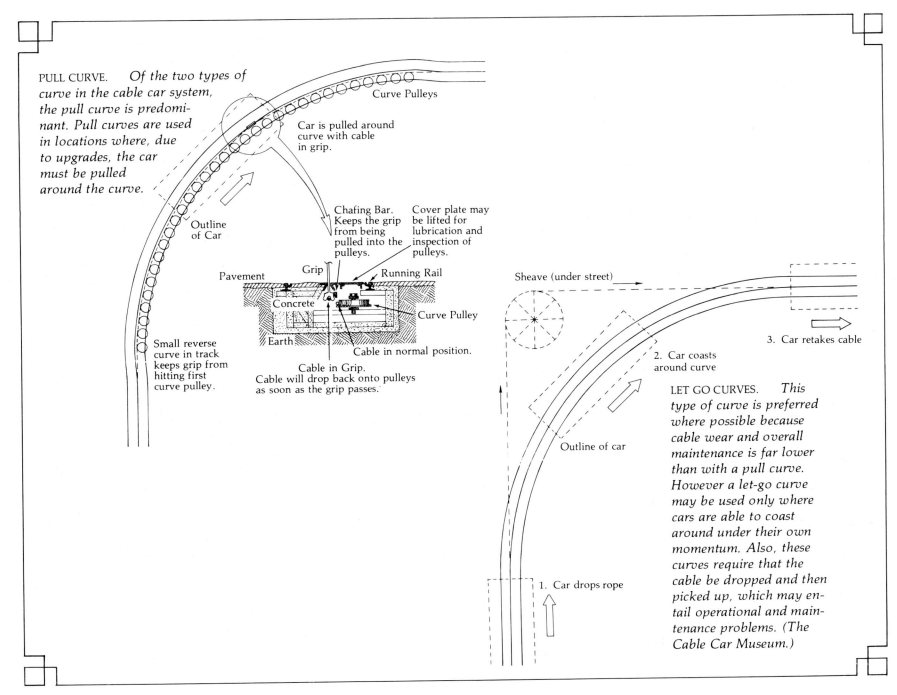

PULL CURVE. *Of the two types of curve in the cable car system, the pull curve is predominant. Pull curves are used in locations where, due to upgrades, the car must be pulled around the curve.*

Curve Pulleys

Car is pulled around curve with cable in grip.

Outline of Car

Chafing Bar. Keeps the grip from being pulled into the pulleys.

Cover plate may be lifted for lubrication and inspection of pulleys.

Pavement

Grip

Running Rail

Concrete

Curve Pulley

Earth

Cable in normal position.

Small reverse curve in track keeps grip from hitting first curve pulley.

Cable in Grip. Cable will drop back onto pulleys as soon as the grip passes.

Sheave (under street)

3. Car retakes cable

2. Car coasts around curve

Outline of car

LET GO CURVES. *This type of curve is preferred where possible because cable wear and overall maintenance is far lower than with a pull curve. However a let-go curve may be used only where cars are able to coast around under their own momentum. Also, these curves require that the cable be dropped and then picked up, which may entail operational and maintenance problems. (The Cable Car Museum.)*

1. Car drops rope

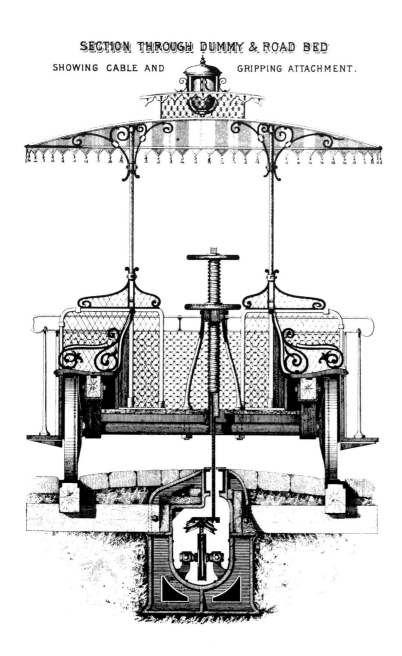

SECTION THROUGH DUMMY & ROAD BED

SHOWING CABLE AND GRIPPING ATTACHMENT.

means of a shank attached to the threaded rod which in turn forced the guide wheels back upon their springs. The cable was grasped and released at will and the movement of the car could be controlled by one man with almost perfect ease. The cable car could not only start smoothly without a sudden jerk, but was also able to stop instantly.

San Francisco's second system, the Sutter Street line, which opened in January of 1877 with 3.5 miles of 5-foot gauge track, used a grip which engaged the cable horizontally from one side. So, too, did the California Street line, which began in April of 1878 with two miles of 3-foot, 6-inch track. But the fourth line on Geary Street, started in March of 1880, reverted to a vertical style of grip.

Of course, the grip is really the core of the cable car. The main foundation is the carry bar which is firmly bolted to the car truck. The principle of engineering employed is simply the lowering and raising of the center plate. As the grip lever is pulled back, the center plate is forced down into the crotch and causes the two hinges to be pushed down between the two rollers. The hinges are wedge-shaped and as they descend, the fixed space between the rollers squeezes them together with a pressure which is proportional to the amount of backward pull on the grip lever. In other words, the harder the gripman pulls on his lever, the tighter the hinges are squeezed together and the cable between the hinges is held firmly. Conversely, when the lever is released forward, the center plate raises the hinges and they separate and release the cable.

An important detail as far as the grip is concerned is the small adjustment lever and rod located well up on the grip lever itself. It is this lever which enables the operator to regulate the movement of the grip and the corresponding pressure of the hinges and dies upon the cable.

Ordinarily the cable is gripped firmly when the grip lever is all the way back. If, however, the cable starts to slip—for example, with an excessive load on a steep hill—the gripman will be tempted to pull back on the grip lever, which will be impossible with the lever already back as far as it will go. To compensate for this condition, as well as to assure room for that extra pull back when just a little more pressure is needed on the cable, the gripman will often take up a few turns on the adjustment rod before he starts up or down a very steep hill. This slight adjustment makes it possible for him to start out with a full grip on the cable and his grip lever but part of the way

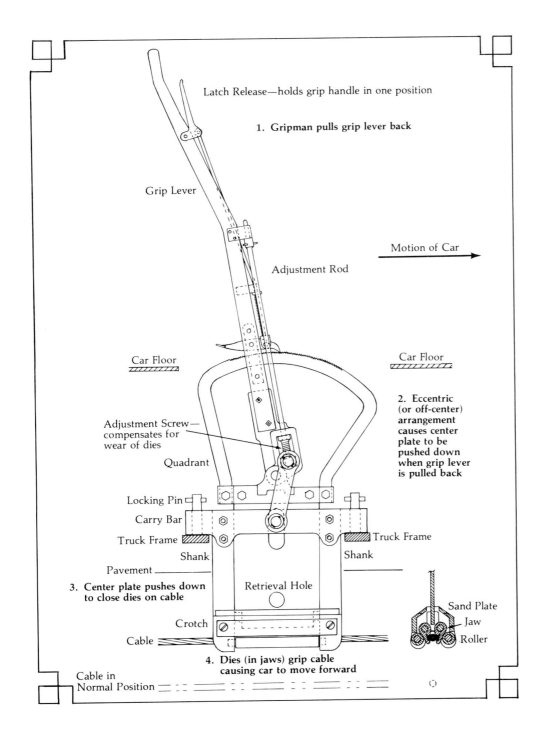

Latch Release—holds grip handle in one position

1. Gripman pulls grip lever back

Grip Lever

Motion of Car →

Adjustment Rod

Car Floor

Car Floor

2. Eccentric (or off-center) arrangement causes center plate to be pushed down when grip lever is pulled back

Adjustment Screw—compensates for wear of dies

Quadrant

Locking Pin

Carry Bar

Truck Frame

Truck Frame

Shank

Shank

Pavement

Retrieval Hole

3. Center plate pushes down to close dies on cable

Crotch

Cable

Sand Plate

Jaw

Roller

4. Dies (in jaws) grip cable causing car to move forward

Cable in Normal Position

Sutter Street Railroad's grip.

ANATOMY OF THE GRIP.   *The grip allows the forward motion of the cable to be transmitted to the car. It works like a vise, gripping the cable more tightly as the gripman pulls back on the lever. The steel dies, the only parts to touch the cable, have a useful life of about four days, less if a new cable has been installed or if traffic is heavy. To replace the dies, the grip must be removed from the car. This is done by removing the locking pins and hoisting the grip up and out through the front door of the car. This type of grip is known as a bottom grip because the cable enters the jaws from beneath. This particular design was invented in 1880 by William Eppelsheimer for the Geary Street, Park & Ocean Railroad. It weighs about 325 pounds. (The Cable Car Museum.)*

ONCE THE CABLE IS IN THE GRIP. *As the grip lever is pulled back, the dies squeeze the cable harder and the car accelerates up to cable speed. Starting is smooth because the cable is lubricated with pine tar which liquefies and then vaporizes under the heat and pressure, ultimately giving a metal-to-metal contact.*

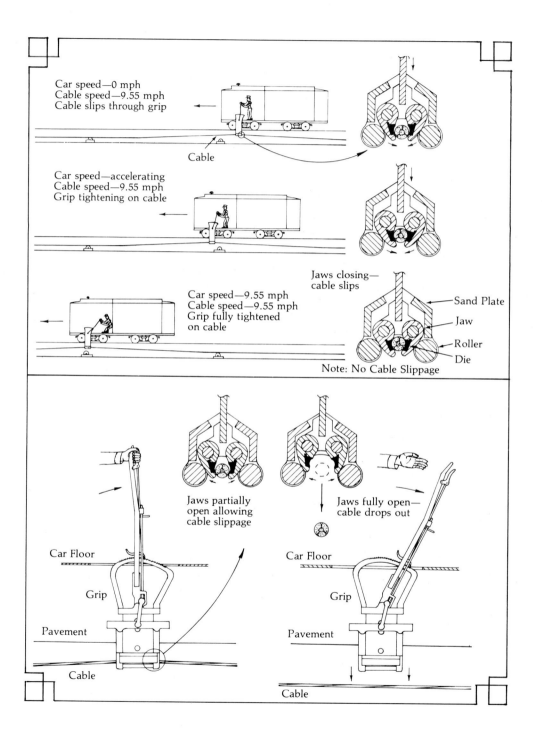

Car speed—0 mph
Cable speed—9.55 mph
Cable slips through grip

Cable

Car speed—accelerating
Cable speed—9.55 mph
Grip tightening on cable

Car speed—9.55 mph
Cable speed—9.55 mph
Grip fully tightened on cable

Jaws closing—cable slips

Sand Plate
Jaw
Roller
Die

Note: No Cable Slippage

NEAR RIGHT. PARTIAL RELEASE. *During passenger and other stops, the grip lever is put about half-way forward, allowing the cable to slip through the grip. This permits stops without having to pick up the cable each time.*

FAR RIGHT. FULL RELEASE. *To drop the cable out of the grip, the grip lever is pushed all the way forward, opening the jaws fully. This is done at cable crossings, switches, let-go curves, and ends of lines. (The Cable Car Museum.)*

Jaws partially open allowing cable slippage

Jaws fully open—cable drops out

Car Floor

Grip

Pavement

Cable

Car Floor

Grip

Pavement

Cable

back. Then if he needs a little more release, he still has room to pull the lever back a bit more. After descending the hill (or climbing it), the gripman simply readjusts the rod back to normal.

According to early public relations announcements, "There are no impediments whatever to the use of the system, either of soil, climate, or temperature." Such announcements often stressed the system's advantages:

1. The steepest grades are as easily worked as levels;
2. The cars may be stopped instantly at any point on the line, and started with promptness and ease;
3. The speed is uniform, and any rate may be established that is desired;
4. The method of working is noiseless and even, and unaccompanied by any annoyance whatever;
5. Perfect cleanliness of the track is secured, an important sanitary element in the system;
6. An unlimited capacity of increase at any time an increased carrying capacity may be required;
7. Perfect freedom from snow blockade, as the power is sufficient at all times to remove the snow as fast as it falls;
8. A simple and economical administration, unattended with unforeseen and unexpected emergencies.

NEAR RIGHT.   *The component parts of a Valencia Street cable car—wheels, running gear and grip. 1889.*

FAR RIGHT.   *The cable car crossing at Geary and Larkin Streets was installed in 1880.*

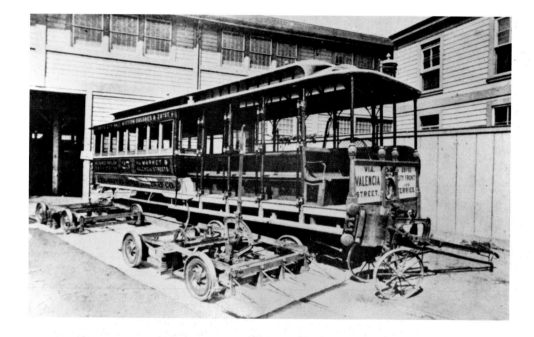

The building of car #505. 1956

THE CABLE CAR COMPANIES AND THEIR LINES

The cable car system was built and developed over a period of 15 years by nine different companies operating a total of 22 lines with some companies operating horsecar lines as well. The little Telegraph Hill Railroad succumbed in 1886, and in 1893 three companies were merged to form the Market Street Railway. Another consolidation in 1902 resulted in United Railroads, which combined the operations of the Market Street Railway, the Sutter Street Railway, and two lines of the newly developed electric trolleys. At the time of the devastating earthquake and fire in April, 1906, four companies operated cable lines, but in the reconstruction of their systems they, for the most part, retained as cable only routes having the most extreme grades, and rebuilt the others for electric traction.

By 1921, when the bankrupt United Railroads was reorganized and the old Market Street Railway name was resurrected, there were two companies operating the remaining cable lines. There were the two lines on Powell Street, the Sacramento-Clay line running over a portion of Hallidie's original route, a segment on the elegant and still gas-lit Pacific Avenue (a route that had no appreciable grades—just powerful residents who wished to preserve a bygone era), a short portion of the once-great Market Street cable system, the unique counterbalance cable-electric operation on Fillmore Hill, and the three lines of the California Street Cable Railroad—California Street, O'Farrell, Jones and Hyde, and the tiny shuttle serving the Tenderloin.

In 1944, Market Street Railway was purchased by the City and County of San Francisco and virtually all the public streetcar, trackless trolley, cable, and motor coach transportation systems were consolidated into the Municipal Railway. The last privately owned transportation company, the California Street Cable Railroad, was taken over by the city in 1954.

Today Muni operates three cable lines, utilizing a total of 38 cars, some of which feature one-hundred-year-old grips, undercarriages and other iron work salvaged after the quake and fire of 1906.

The California Street line runs east and west from Market and Drumm Streets to Van Ness Avenue, while a portion of Cal Cable's old O'Farrell, Jones and Hyde line (the original "Hyde Street Grip") survives as part of the route followed by one of the two north-south lines running from the turntable at Powell and Market to Fisherman's Wharf and Aquatic Park.

The Clay Street Hill Railroad, September 1873, a week after revenue service began. The man standing between the dummy and the trailer has sometimes been identified as Hallidie himself.

Clay Street Hill Railroad

Hallidie's plan had been to construct his pioneering cable road on California Street, but soon he shifted the site of his "experiment" two blocks to the north. The original, passenger-carrying cable railroad, Clay Street, was popular and successful because of its location near the downtown area and because it easily climbed the steep Nob Hill and made accessible sparsely populated areas beyond.

The cable-train consisted of two small cars—an open "dummy" or grip car pulling a trailer that was usually closed. The dummy was not originally designed to carry passengers, but when the line was officially opened to the public on September 1, 1873, the area occupied by the grip mechanism and its operator was flanked by wooden benches, providing seating for 16 people, while the trail car was designed to carry 14. However, trains were observed carrying as many as 70, and "hanging from a cable car," now closely regulated, became *de rigueur* for residents and visitors alike.

The 3-foot, 6-inch gauge double track ascended 307 feet over a distance of about one-half mile from the double turntables at Kearny Street to the powerhouse at Leavenworth. In 1877, the track was extended to Van Ness Avenue, making the line just under a mile long.

The "endless" wire rope, manufactured by Hallidie's own California Wire Works, had a total length of 11,000 feet and was supported every 39 feet on 11-inch sheaves. The motive power for the cable was supplied by a steam engine at the powerhouse. It initially operated the cable at 4 mph, and then was speeded up to 6.

The grip was Hallidie's screw-within-a-screw that grasped the cable on the bottom of a horizontal vise.

On September 8, 1888, the company was bought by Ferries & Cliff House Railroad which incorporated the route into its Sacramento-Clay line. By 1891, the original double track on Clay Street had been superceded by F&CH's single track and the pioneer road was discontinued. The Sacramento-Clay line was converted to diesel buses on February 15, 1942.

Sutter Street Railroad

The versatile blacksmith and inventor Henry Casebolt began converting his horsecar line to cable in the mid-1870s. On January 27, 1877, the city's second cable line began service. It ran along Sutter from the intersection of Market, Sutter and Sansome Streets to the powerhouse at Larkin and Bush. In 1878, a branch crosstown line was opened, running along Larkin between the powerhouse and Hayes Street, and in 1879 the main line was extended west along Sutter to Central (now Presidio) Avenue, where another car

APR. 1885 7

SUTTER ST. R.R.Co.
TRANSFER

SUTTER STREET
TO
POLK STREET.
GOOD FOR THIS TRIP ONLY

TRANSFERS ISSUED AND
RECEIVED-ONLY AT
THE POINT OF CHANGE.
A.K.STEVENS Sect.

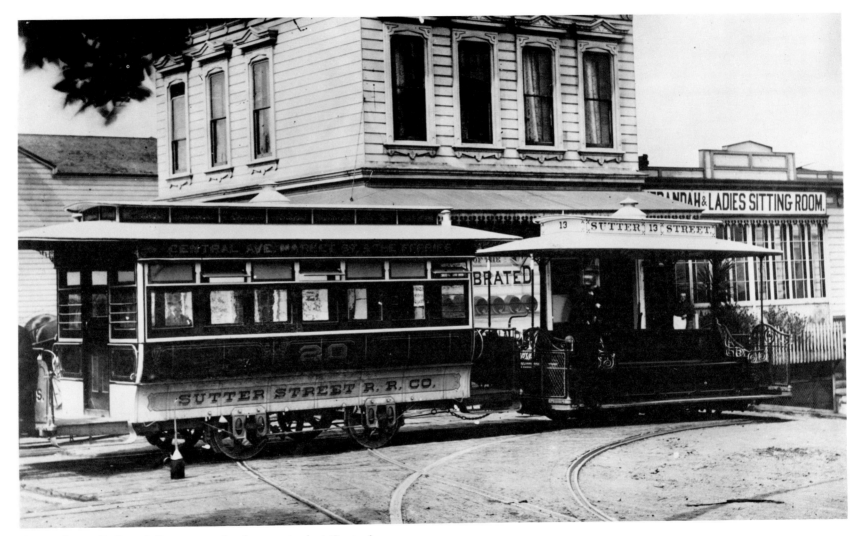

Sutter Street Railroad Company. At the terminal at Central
(Presidio) Avenue and Sutter, 1890.

California Street Cable Railroad, 1882. It's been said that the passengers on this car include Adolph Sutro (holding the trailer grabiron) and Mark Twain (in silhouetted profile on the dummy).

house was built. In 1883, under new ownership, the company consolidated its operations into a new powerhouse at Sutter and Polk, and began to push the branch line south along Ninth to Brannan, and north to Pacific Avenue and out Pacific to Divisadero. Around 1887, the company's name was changed from "Railroad" to "Railway."

The system's 5-foot gauge double track was extensively rebuilt in the early 1890s. The completed system had about six miles of line. The company had wanted to convert the line of horsecar track that connected the main line to the Ferry Building, but it never did.

The Sutter Street Railroad used a grip mechanism designed by Asa Hovey, a foreman in Casebolt's machine works. It was a lever operated grip that grasped the cable from the side. This mechanism employed a lever in place of the screw and wheel to clamp vertically on the cable, which moved at a speed of approximately 8 mph. This was the most common grip used until the Market Street Cable Railway began operation in August, 1883.

The company was absorbed into the United Railroads in 1902 and the lines continued to operate until the earthquake in 1906, after which the system—with the exception of the extension along Pacific Avenue—was converted to electric traction. The successor company to the United Railroads, Market Street Railways, discontinued the Pacific Avenue line on November 29, 1929.

California Street Cable Railroad

Leland Stanford, impressed by the success of Hallidie's Clay Street Hill Railroad, set his sights on California Street, the street on which he had built his mansion and the street Hallidie himself had originally selected as the location for his cable line. In 1876, together with several of his associates in the Central Pacific Railroad, Stanford secured a franchise and entrusted the design of the new road to Henry Root.

On April 12, 1878, the *Morning Call* reported:

over 11,000 persons were carried over the California Street Railroad Wednesday (April 10, 1878), the opening day. Passengers were greatly pleased with the elegance of the cars and dummies.

The route paralleled the Clay Street route up and over Nob Hill, but was the first line to extend cable service into the Western Addition beyond Van Ness, which it did in 1879.

In 1891, the company under new ownership, built a crosstown line on O'Farrell, Jones and Hyde Street, and a shuttle along Jones serving the Tenderloin. It was the last cable line built in the city.

The system's lines covered 11 miles of narrow gauge (3.6 feet) track. The line on California Street was straight while the Hyde line contained a number of curves and runs on different streets before terminating at Beach Street. Both lines had a number of steep grades, some as high as 620 feet and having a 21 percent grading. The two lines utilized four 1¼-inch radius ropes with an average life of about 12 months and a total length of 11¼ miles. They were moved at an average speed of 8 mph by an 182 horsepower steam engine located in the powerhouse at California and Hyde.

The California Street line employed a side grip, designed by Root, that had the rope on one side only. Hyde Street, with its 22 rope drops during the course of a round trip, utilized the Eppelsheimer bottom grip which was considered more efficient in this situation, although it was somewhat harder on the rope. This line's steep grades, many curves and rope drops, and the dazzling views of the bay it afforded its passengers, inspired Gelett Burgess to write "The Ballad of the Hyde Street Grip" which was published in 1901.

Throw her off at Powell Street, let her go out Post,
Watch her well at Geary and at Sutter when you coast!
Easy at the Power House, have a care at Clay,
Sacramento, Washington, Jackson—all the way!
Drop your rope at Union—never make a slip—
The lever keeps you busy, on the Hyde Street Grip!

In 1888, the California Street Cable Railroad Company commissioned a local car builder, the John Hammond Car Company, to develop a new type of car that combined the grip car and trailer into one unit. The new car, which appeared in 1889, had a grip section at each end and a closed section in the middle. It was able to operate from either end and eliminated the need for turntables or other cumbersome switching devices at the ends of the

The first "California type" cable car. Because of its size, it was soon nicknamed Jumbo, after the elephant of P. T. Barnum fame.

*Geary Street, Park & Ocean Railroad. At Geary and
Presidio Avenue, 1890, with Calvary Cemetery in the background. Here passengers could disembark to picnic in one
of the four cemeteries clustered near Lone Mountain, or
transfer to a steam dummy train which would take them to
Golden Gate Park. On the site of this cemetery today is a
Sears department store and a mosaic of undulating little
streets serving a pleasant residential neighborhood.*

34

lines. The new car was an immediate success and the California Street company soon replaced all of their small cable trains with this new type of car, which became known as the "California" type. These combination cars, 30 feet long and weighing 11,200 pounds, were designed to carry 34 passengers in both the open and closed sections, although they had been known to carry as many as 120.

The company was extremely successful, and though it suffered considerable damage in the earthquake and fire (of its rolling stock only one old dummy car survived) the grades along its lines made replacement by electric traction impossible, and the two lines, plus the Jones Street shuttle, were restored.

The company, which had remained independent while other cable companies merged and consolidated, was bought by the City and County of San Francisco's Municipal Railway in the early 1950s. The Jones Street shuttle and the O'Farrell-Jones-Hyde line were discontinued, and the California Street line ceased to run beyond Van Ness. However, in April of 1957, the new Powell-Hyde line was opened, which operates today along a spectacular portion of the route traveled by the original Hyde Street Grip.

Geary Street, Park & Ocean Railroad

Geary Street, with no serious grades, was the city's principal east-west thoroughfare. Charles F. Crocker, son of one of the four founders of the Central Pacific Railroad, opened cable car operations on Geary Street in February, 1880. The line ran from Lotta's Fountain at the intersection of Geary, Market and Kearny Streets to the powerhouse at Buchanan and then out to Central (Presidio) Avenue. In 1892, the line, by then owned by the Market Street Railway, was extended to Golden Gate Park at 5th Avenue and Fulton Street.

The line originally employed the Eppelsheimer bottom grip, and the double track was five feet in gauge. When the Market Street Railway extended the line, it converted the grip to the Root single-jaw side grip, and the track to 4-foot, 8½-inch gauge. The plan had been to be able to run the Geary Street cars on down Market Street to the Ferry Building, but the Geary line continued to terminate at Lotta's Fountain.

After the quake and fire, the line resumed operation but was closed in 1912 to make way for Municipal Railway's electric service.

Presidio & Ferries Railroad

Running out Union Street, this line was the first to tackle Russian Hill. It opened on October 23, 1880, with double track of 5-foot gauge and utilizing a grip similar to Hallidie's hollow screw mechanism used on the Clay Street hill. The cable speed was almost 7 mph, powered out of a plant on Leaven-worth Street.

The first let-go curve was installed to move the cars from Union onto Montgomery (now Columbus) Avenue so that the line could serve the central business district, but it never got further than the present intersection of Columbus Avenue and Montgomery Street. Its ferry-bound passengers made connection with a horsecar line running on Jackson and Washington Streets.

In the early 1890s the line was extended to the Presidio along Union, Baker and Lombard Streets. The extension included a pull curve, and certain aspects of the original technology were modified, particularly the Hallidie bottom grip, by John C. H. Stut.

The line was converted to electricity in 1906.

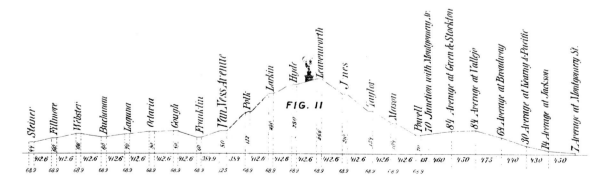

Presidio and Ferries Railroad Company, 1891. This company (also known as the Union Street line) had but one route with a short branch to Harbor View Park. Nevertheless, it utilized horsecars and a steam streetcar as well as cable cars.

MARKET ST. CABLE RY. CO.	CASTRO ST. LINE	0ϕ	0ϕ	0ϕ	0ϕ	0ϕ	0ϕ	0ϕ	0ϕ	0ϕ	0ϕ	0ϕ	SF & S M RY. (East).
		1	2	3	4	5	6	7	8	9	10	11 12	
		02	02	02	02	02	02	02	02	02	02	02	Haight St (West).
		THIS CHECK NOT TRANSFERABLE. It will not be honored unless received by the holder from Conductor of connecting car and presented within the time and upon the line for which issued—as indicated by punch marks.										*S. Willer* Secy.	Turk St.
		GOOD ONLY AT MEETING POINT WITH TRANSFER LINE.											Fifth or Powell St
		VOID UNI S USED AUG. 29		A M	20	20	20	20		20	20		
					6	7	8	9	10	11	12		Geary St
					40	40	40	40	40	40	40		

Market Street Cable Railway Company

In 1883, the Market Street Cable Railway Company, known locally as the Southern Pacific line because its supporters included Charles Crocker and Henry E. Huntington of the Southern Pacific Company, opened the first line of the system that was to become the city's most extensive. They ran along San Francisco's main shopping street—Market—and radiated out into residential areas not served by other companies.

Henry Root designed the system, employing his single-jaw side grip. The track was 4-foot, 8½-inch gauge.

The Valencia Street line ran from the Ferry Building down Market and out Valencia Street through the Mission District to 28th and Valencia Streets. Soon branch lines off Market ran out both McAllister and Haight Streets to Golden Gate Park. In 1886, another line to the park along Hayes Street was opened. The company's fifth and last line, which began operation in 1887, ran from the main powerhouse at Market, Valencia and Haight to Castro and 26th Streets to ascend the only steep grades on the system.

Market Street became the trunk line of the entire cable system, with virtually all lines branching off from it, and the areas south of it became known as "South of the Slot." Activity at the "hub"—the Ferry Building—was intense in the early 1890s. During rush hours the headway of cars on lower Market Street was only 15 seconds. The turntable at the terminal had the capacity to handle two cars at once.

The company used new Root-designed combination cars, reconstructed horsecars with dummies, cars that were open at only one end, and cars that were completely open-air.

The cables were run from three powerhouses. The total length of 181,600 feet of cable was driven at speeds ranging from 8 to 10 mph.

In 1893 the Southern Pacific Company arranged a merger of the Market Street Cable Railway, the Omnibus Railroad & Cable Company, the Ferries & Cliff House Railway and two horsecar operations. The new company was known as the Market Street Railway. In 1902, another merger resulted in the United Railroads of San Francisco.

All the lines were electrified after the earthquake and fire, with the exception of the Castro Street line between 18th and 26th Streets, which was retained, because of steep grades, until April 7, 1942.

Market Street Cable Railway Company. A cable car of the
Valencia Street line at Hayes and Market, 1880s.

*Ferries & Cliff House Railway. At the Market
and Powell Street "turn-around" in 1889.
(Robert Schlaich Collection.)*

Telegraph Hill Railroad

This tiny, short-lived line, which opened in 1884, ran up Greenwich Street from Powell to a fantastic, turreted wooden "castle"—the Pioneer Park Observatory—at the top of Telegraph Hill. This line operated as a funicular railway—the ascending car and the descending car counterbalanced each other in weight. While other systems employed double sets of track, the three cars of the Telegraph Hill line ran on a single track with pullouts to allow another car to pass. Operation of the line was discontinued after a disastrous wreck in 1886.

Ferries & Cliff House Railway

In the mid-1880s a project of the powerful Sutro family—the Park & Cliff House Railway—was sold to W. J. Adams, who had been promoting a project of his own, the Powell Street Railway. The Sutros' plan for the east-west line had been to connect, by a combination of cable and steam dummy, the Ferry Building to their Cliff House resort area overlooking the Pacific Ocean. Adams' line went from Powell and Market north over Nob Hill to Bay and Taylor Streets near Fisherman's Wharf, and he continued to call it the Powell Street Railway, despite the new corporate name.

 The design of the complicated new system, with its two dissimilar lines operating out of one powerhouse, was entrusted to Howard C. Holmes, who had designed the powerhouse for the Oakland Cable Railway across the bay. The tracks were narrow gauge, 3-feet, 6-inches, and Holmes utilized the Eppelsheimer bottom grip, chiefly because Powell Street, being an inferior line, had many rope drops, as well as a let-go curve at Mason and Jackson.

 The powerhouse, which operated the cable at a little over 9 mph, was located on Mason between Washington and Jackson—the site of the powerhouse which operates today's remaining lines.

 The east-west line went along Washington and Jackson to a turntable at Central (Presidio) and California. In the early 1890s, the original Clay Street Hill line was incorporated into a third line of F&CH, and this ran from a

Telegraph Hill Railroad. Ascending Greenwich Street, 1885.

turntable at the Ferry Building west on Clay to Central, and back again east on Sacramento. The total length of the three lines was approximately seven miles.

In 1893 the company was merged into the Market Street Railway and in the following year the Sacramento line was extended to Golden Gate Park via Lake and 6th Avenue to the site of the Midwinter Fair of 1894. In 1902 United Railroads took over, and in 1906 the powerhouse and much of the equipment was demolished. However, the lines of the former F&CH included grades that were impossible to convert to electric traction, so they were re-established, in whole or in part, as cable.

Today, the Powell-Mason line to Fisherman's Wharf remains unchanged, while the Powell-Hyde line to Aquatic Park contains a portion of the Washington-Jackson route as well as the route of original Hyde Street Grip of Cal Cable's O'Farrell, Jones, and Hyde line. The Sacramento-Clay line was converted to buses in February 1942.

Omnibus Railroad & Cable Company

The last cable company formed in San Francisco had a complex and extensive system, second only in mileage to the Market Street Cable Railroad, but it was the least successful.

The main line, which began operation in 1888, ran from the Ferry Building out Howard Street to 26th Street, with a branch on 24th Street running east to Potrero Avenue. The Post Street cable began at Market and Montgomery and ran to the powerhouse at 10th and Howard. The Ellis Street line, the only route with grades of any consequence, ran from Market to Golden Gate Park at Haight and Stanyan. The line on Oak Street ran from the powerhouse to the same destination as the Ellis Street line, although its route was straight.

The company used an Eppelsheimer grip, because of the inferior position of its cables, which moved the cars at about 10 mph, except along the Post Street segment where the cars ran at 8.5 mph. By the end of the century, all the lines had been abandoned, or converted to electric traction.

Omnibus Railroad & Cable Company. At 24th Street and Potrero Avenue in the 1890s. The horsecar in the background belonged to the same company and ran out Potrero Avenue.

THE FIRST ONE HUNDRED YEARS

RIGHT. This could be the earliest photograph of Hallidie's pioneering cable car. The grip (dummy) car at the inner terminus of the line at Clay and Kearny, August 1873.

FAR RIGHT. The Clay and Kearny turntables, 1870s. Note the stairs used to enter the "bobtailed" cars. Portsmouth Square is to the right.

Clay Street and Van Ness Avenue, 1877.

Larkin and Clay Streets. 1879.

ABOVE.   *Headed toward Van Ness Avenue on Clay Street, late 1870s.*

RIGHT.   *Chinatown, 1875. A Clay Street cable car approaches Dupont (Grant) Avenue. (The Bancroft Library.)*

FAR RIGHT.   *A Sutter Street cable train at Sutter and Larkin in the 1880s. This photograph is unusual because it is the only one of a San Francisco grip car hauling more than one trailer, and because all the passengers are women—the only men on board being the conductor and gripman.*

LEFT. *A Sutter Street grip-and-trailer passes Temple Emanu-El Between Powell and Stockton Streets, 1880s. The temple was destroyed in 1906; the 450 Sutter Medical-Dental Building stands on the site today. (The Bancroft Library)*

BELOW. *A somewhat later cable train on the same street but headed the other way. The trees next door to Emanu-El (center right) have given way to buildings.*

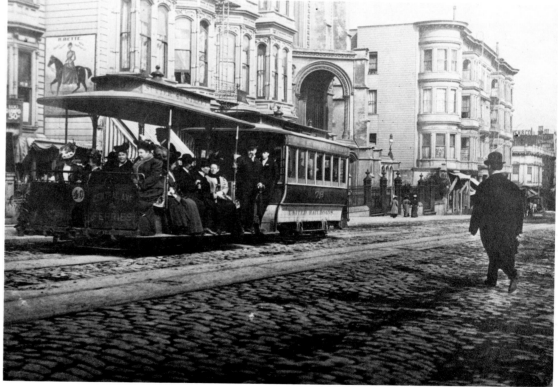

Sutter Street cable dummy, Sutter and Powell Streets, 1905.

FAR LEFT. *The main intersection of the Sutter Street Railway at Sutter and Polk, 1890s. Here its east-west Central Avenue bound line, crossed its 9th, Larkin, Polk, Pacific line. The signal stand, to the left of the lamp post, had a small lamp of its own on top and warned gripmen of an approaching train.*

LEFT. *Three blocks away, Sutter Street's Polk-Larkin crosstown line intersected the Geary Street line. 1890s.*

BELOW. *In 1888 the Sutter Street Railway pushed its crosstown line out Pacific Avenue west to Divisadero.*

The extension along Pacific Avenue, looking west from the corner of Pacific and Pierce, 1896.

54

California Street Cable Railroad car and powerhouse prior to 1891.

*California Street and Central (Presidio) Avenue, the western terminus of the
California Street cable, 1880s.*

California Street looking east from Powell, 1880s. Kearny Street horsecar crossing in the distance. Cars below Kearny are horsecars.

Looking up California Street from the heart of the financial district before the line was extended to Market Street in 1890 (there are horsecar tracks in the foreground but no cable slot). Center left, is the Merchant's Exchange. Beyond can be seen Old St. Mary's Church and the Hopkins mansion at the top of Nob Hill. (Taber Photos.)

59

The Mark Hopkins mansion, California Street, 1890s. Hopkins died in 1878 and never occupied his vainglorious palace. Eventually it was presented to the San Francisco Art Association to be utilized for its school. In the 1920s the Mark Hopkins Hotel was built on the site. (The Bancroft Library.)

LEFT.   *Senator James G. ("Slippery Jim") Fair, a Comstock baron and one of the nabobs, acquired a large lot on California Street with the intention of building a mansion that would rival Hopkins'. He died before the plans were completed and his daughters erected the neo-Renaissance Fairmont Hotel instead.*

BELOW.   *Inside the signal booth at the corner of California and Powell. The right-of-way at this intersection is still controlled from this tiny gazebo. (The San Francisco Public Library.)*

The Fairmont Hotel, and at left, the Flood mansion. Now the Pacific Union Club, the Flood is the only nabob mansion remaining. To the left, out of the picture, were the edifices of Huntington (now a park) and Crocker (where Grace Cathedral stands today). (Louis Stein Collection.)

62

Another view of the Flood, after the earthquake and before the Pacific Union Club remodeled it. A Sacramento Street cable car is in the foreground. (Marilyn Blaisdell Collection.)

ABOVE.   The other major line of Cal Street Cable, the
O'Farrell, Jones and Hyde line, at O'Farrell and Stockton
Streets. Spreckels Building on Market, center right. (The
Bancroft Library.)

RIGHT.   The original "Hyde Street Grip." The cobbles and
weedy dirt paths have been replaced by pavement and side-
walks, but the Tudor-style house remains today on the corner of Hyde and Francisco Streets. (The Bancroft Library.)

FAR RIGHT.   Looking east from Russian Hill, about 1885.
In the foreground, lower right, is a Powell Street line cable
car running along Mason. In the background, left, is the
Pioneer Park Observatory atop Telegraph Hill, the terminus of the short-lived Telegraph Hill Railroad.

LEFT.   *All three cars of the Telegraph Hill Railroad on Greenwich Street. (Taber Photo.)*

BELOW.   *Pioneer Park Observatory, Telegraph Hill. 1880s.*

ABOVE.   *Geary Street cable crossing Kearny at Lotta's Fountain—the end of its line. 1885.*

RIGHT.   *Geary cable passing Union Square on the left, two weeks before the earthquake in 1906. The steel frame of the building under construction survived the quake, but work on it was not resumed for several years. It became known as the "bird-cage building." Eventually it was completed and it stands today.*

Grand Hotel.

HIBERNIA BANK.

PALACE HOTEL.

San Francisco, Cal.

New Building designed for

BRADLEY & RULOFSON'S ART GALLERY.

"At the end of the trail is the Palace." The famous old hotel, rebuilt in 1909, continued to use this motto which harked back to the days of the Overland Trail. A
Geary Street cable crosses Grant Avenue—the street that had been called Dupont
until shortly before the turn of the century. (Louis Stein Collection.)

70

LEFT.   *Presidio & Ferries Railroad's Union Street line at Montgomery (now Columbus) Avenue and Jackson Street. Here passengers transferred to horsecars which would take them to the ferries.*

UPPER RIGHT.   *Union Street. 1880s. (Louis Stein Collection.)*

LOWER RIGHT.   *Horsecars, in United Railroads livery, at the Ferry Building. Early 1900s. (B. H. Ward Collection.)*

ABOVE.   Before the advent of cable cars on Market Street, steam cars operated along the first tracks laid down in the city for a street railway. The steam cars were ousted in 1868, and were replaced by horsecars. This car, at Market and Montgomery, was headed for Woodward's Gardens on Valencia Street, which was described by Watkins and Olmsted in Mirror of the Dream as a "Victorian Disneyland."

LEFT.   Looking east down Market Street in 1863, toward the old Ferry Building and Goat (Yerba Buena) Island. Hallidie's invention was eight years in the future and cable slots along this major thoroughfare did not appear until 1883. (The Bancroft Library.)

RIGHT.   Market and Fourth Streets, looking up Ellis. A pre-cable view of Market Street on a rainy day.

Looking west on Market. Right of center is the intersection of Montgomery, Post and Market Streets; to the left is the old Palace Hotel. The tracks are for horse-cars; the distinctive slot, indicating a cable line, is nowhere in evidence. (The Bancroft Library.)

*The cables come to Market Street, 1880s. The de Young Building, home of the
San Francisco* Chronicle, *stood at the corner of Kearny and Market, just beyond
the Geary Street cable's turntable and Lotta's Fountain. Across Market, on the
corner of Third Street, was the home of one of the* Chronicle's *rival newspapers,
Hearst's* Examiner *(right).*

LEFT. *The original powerhouse of the great Market Street Cable Railway system, Valencia and Market. The steam dummy train in foreground was an extension out Market to Castro, later a cable line. (The Bancroft Library.)*

ABOVE. *A McAllister car of the Market Street Cable Railway at the line's car barn and powerhouse, 1885.*

RIGHT. *Market Street, turn of the century. Left of center is the Emporium—self-styled "California's largest and America's greatest" department store. In the distance is San Francisco's first skyscraper, the Spreckels Building, also known as the Call Building and, more recently, Central Tower.*

Market Street, late 1890s. Second Street on the left, the Crocker Building, at the intersection of Post, Montgomery and Market, on the right. (Railway Negative Exchange.)

LEFT.   E. J. "Lucky" Baldwin's sumptuous hotel, on the corner of Powell and Market next to the Powell Street turntable.

BELOW.   Two Powell Street cable cars at the turntable in front of the smoldering remains of the Baldwin Hotel, 1898. "Lucky" Baldwin was unlucky this time—he was uninsured, and the tragic fire cost him his Comstock fortune. (Louis Stein Collection.)

A circus parade making its way up Market from the Ferry Building to the
grounds at Ninth Street. Elephants pass the site where the Baldwin once stood,
and where the Flood Building stands today. Right of center is the old five-story
Phelan Building on the corner of Grant, and the clock tower of the de Young
Building at Kearny. (B. H. Ward Collection.)

A patriotic celebration on Market, early 1900s. The Phelan, Mutual Bank, and Chronicle (de Young) Buildings on the left, the Spreckels (Central Tower) on the right.

ABOVE.   *A Market Street Cable Railway car of the Valencia Street line, 1880s.*

RIGHT.   *A Valencia Street cable passing over construction work entailing repairs to a complicated switch at Hayes Street. (Louis Stein Collection.)*

FAR RIGHT.   *Market Street's Haight Line. Two cars at the turntable, Haight and Stanyan. 1890s. (Robert Schlaich Collection.)*

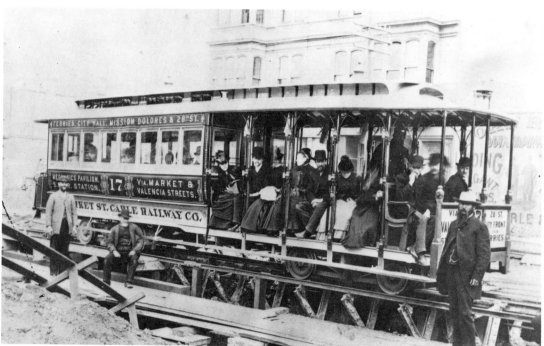

ABOVE.   *On the turntable at the entrance to Golden Gate Park, Haight and Stanyan Streets, early 1900s.*

LEFT.   *A group portrait of Market Street Cable Railway carmen. Haight Street carbarn, 1890s.*

RIGHT.   *A Haight Street cable heading up Market from the old Ferry Building, 1880s.*

In the early 1880s all rail traffic to the Ferry Building at the foot of Market on East Street (the Embarcadero) was horsecar. Market Street Cable Railway, in 1883, was the first to establish a cable line to the ferry terminal.

Ferry Building, 1890s. (Railway Negative Exchange.)

Waiting for cable car connections in front of the Ferry Building, turn-of-the century.

The waiting room, old Ferry Building, early 1890s.

ABOVE.   *Market Street Post Office and mail car at Golden Gate Park. Haight and Stanyan Streets. Several cable and electric lines carried mail from outlying postal stations to the mail dock at the Ferry Building.*

RIGHT.   *The mail car of the Sacramento Street cable line idles in front of the construction of the new ferry terminal with an electric mail car and a horsecar of the Presidio & Ferries Railroad. 1897.*

RIGHT. *Looking up Market Street from the Ferry Building during the afternoon rush hour, August 1905.*

BELOW. *Market Street cable cars on the double turntable at the new Ferry Building. (The Bancroft Library.)*

FAR RIGHT. *The new Ferry Building, a San Francisco landmark of today. This photograph shows pedestrian, streetcar, automobile, and cable car traffic at rush hour in the 1920s.*

ABOVE.   *Castro Street cable at 26th and Castro Streets, 1890. This was the last extension of the great Market Street system.*

RIGHT.   *The Castro Street hill. (The Bancroft Library.)*

LEFT.   *Market and Castro Streets, 1890s. The children are scrambling for election cards being tossed from the cable car by a campaigning politician. Election cards were as avidly collected in those days as were the baseball cards of more recent times.*

BELOW.   *This open cable car ran on the Castro Street line until the mid-1920s at which time it was rebuilt into a standard open-and-closed model.*

RIGHT.   *Another open car, Valencia line.*

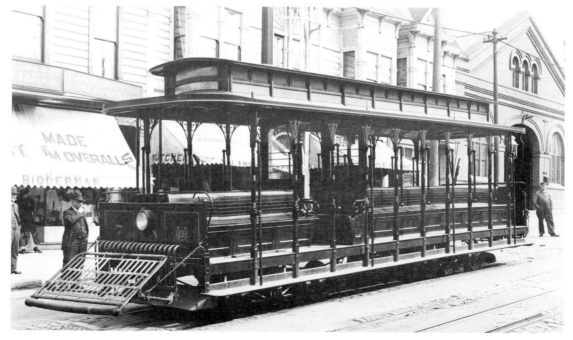

UPPER LEFT. *The Washington and Mason car barn and powerhouse of the Powell Street line as it appeared in 1888. (Richard Schlaich Collection.)*

LOWER LEFT. *Looking down a weedy Washington Street before the earthquake. The stack of the powerhouse on Mason Street is center left. (The Bancroft Library.)*

RIGHT. *A Sacramento cable at 6th Avenue and Fulton Street in 1898, after F&CH was absorbed by the new Market Street Railway. This car still runs today, as #6 of the Powell-Mason line. (Louis Stein Collection.)*

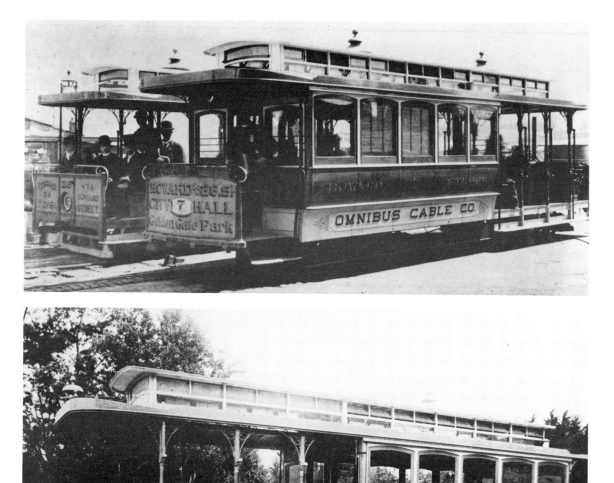

UPPER RIGHT.   Omnibus Cable Company was
the last company to build a cable system, and
the least successful. It had four lines, none of
which survived into the 20th century. Here are
cars of the Howard Street line on the turntable
at 26th and Howard, 1890s.

LOWER RIGHT.   A car of Omnibus Cable's Ellis
line on the turntable at Golden Gate Park,
1890s.

FAR RIGHT.   Omnibus' Post Street line crosses
the tracks of Market Street's McAllister line. The
turreted building is Prager's Department Store,
on the corner of Market and Jones, which adver-
tised "Carmen's Uniforms and Outfits, complete
in every detail." In the foreground can be seen
the lamp posts and shrubbery of the old City
Hall complex.

STERLING FURNITURE CO. CARPETS.

FURNITURE STORED EASTERN PLAN.

YOSEMITE HOUSE. FURNISHED ROOMS

YOSEMITE HOUSE LODGINGS.

THE FISCHER

NEW CITY HALL. Lunch & Sample Parlors.

LEFT.   *McAllister Street cable switching out of Market to run along the*
northern side of Civic Center, 1880s.

A McAllister Street cable passing in front of St. Ignatius Church and College, the Hall of Records in the background. Nearby was the City Hall which took almost thirty years to build. While its promoters claimed it was to be "the largest and most durable structure," cynics were calling it the "new City Hall ruin." And a ruin it soon was. (Oakland Public Library.)

LEFT. *Earthquake and fire, April 18, 1906. The Washington-Mason powerhouse was half-rubble immediately following the quake.*

ABOVE. *After the fire, the powerhouse was virtually a total loss though somehow the stack resisted toppling. (The Bancroft Library.)*

LEFT.   *Union Street cable tracks after the earthquake, looking west from Steiner Street.*

RIGHT.   *A burnt car lies crumpled on Pacific Avenue.*

110

LEFT.   *Reconstruction of the Washington and Mason Street powerhouse, March 2, 1907. The steam indicates that operation of some lines had been reinstated. Cars were stored outdoors during barn reconstruction.*

ABOVE.   *The only piece of California Cable's equipment to survive the fire. All the other cars of the company burned at Hyde Street. (The Bancroft Library.)*

RIGHT.   *When California Street Cable Railroad resumed service, new cars were so urgently needed that they appeared in primer paint. The beautiful maroon, cream and blue livery with the elaborate gold leaf striping and lettering was applied to the cars as soon as conditions returned to normal.*

FAR LEFT.   When electric cars replaced the Market Street cables following the earthquake and fire, many of the old cable cars, stripped of their wheels and running gear, were used as dwellings for people made homeless by the disaster. This group, photographed in 1908, was in the Richmond district, California Street and 5th Avenue.

LEFT.   California and Grant Avenue, 1908. (The Bancroft Library.)

BELOW.   A Powell Street cable car in United Railroad livery, 1908. This car is still running today.

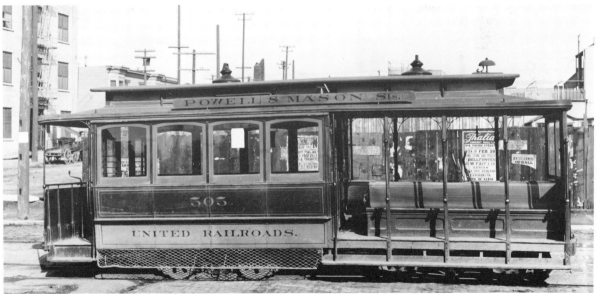

ABOVE.   *California and Montgomery Streets, about 1910. The city had made a surprisingly fast recovery from the earthquake and fire. (Railway Negative Exchange.)*

RIGHT.   *Looking up Geary from Lotta's Fountain at Kearny Street, 1910. (Randolph Brandt Collection.)*

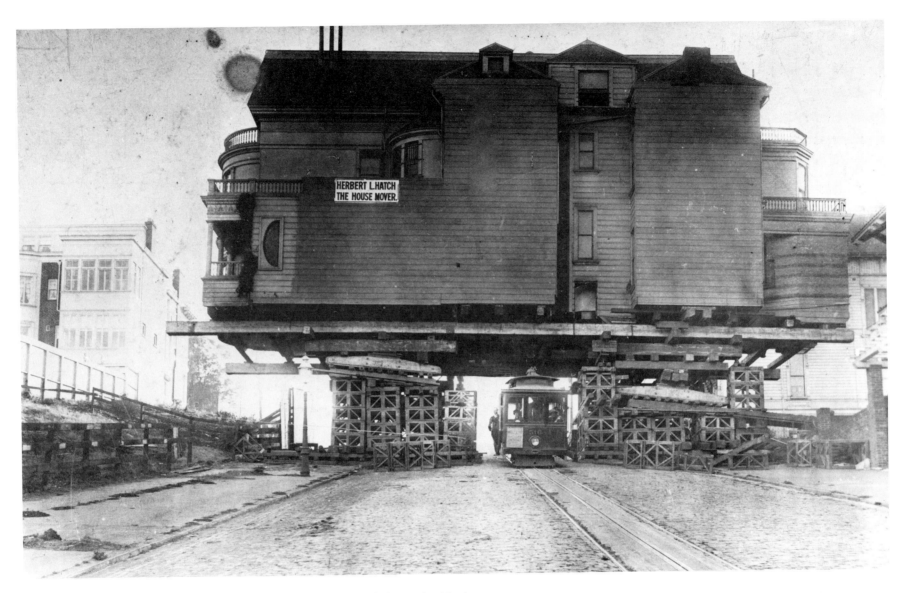

LEFT. *Geary Street turntable, 1910. This car was inherited from the Market and Hayes line after that line was superceded by electric cars following the earthquake and fire.*

ABOVE. *This large house was moved down a 16.5 percent grade on Washington Street while cable traffic continued uninterrupted beneath it, 1913.*

LEFT.   *A Washington and Jackson line cable car, 1914.*
This car is still in use today.

RIGHT.   *This unique one-man cable car was an unsuccessful experiment of United Railroad in 1915. After only a few days of use along Pacific Avenue, the car was removed from service, and the usual two-man cars were reinstated.*

BELOW.   *A Sacramento-Clay cable car returning from the Elkton Yard after a new paint job. The cable car is being towed over electric lines by a trolley. 1929.*

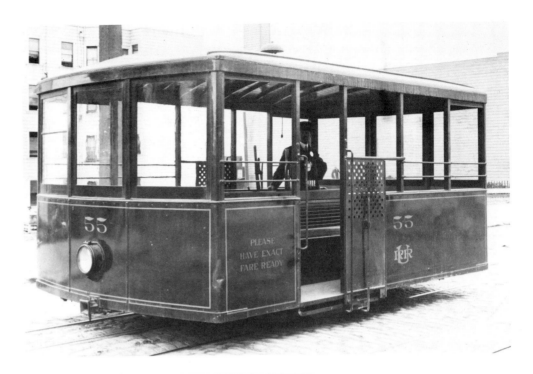

LEFT.   *A public wake for the venerable Pacific Avenue cable car line on its last day of operation, November 17, 1929.*

ABOVE.   *Another wake, almost 12 years later, for the Castro Street cables, which were draped in black on their last day, April 5, 1941.*

RIGHT.   *This energetic demonstration was to no avail, and on May 15, 1954, the O'Farrell, Jones and Hyde Street line ran for the last time. (San Francisco Public Library.)*

In 1938, a Sutter Street cable train, dating back to the 1870s, was refurbished for the 1939 World's Fair at Treasure Island. It is now on display at the Cable Car Museum at Washington and Mason Streets.

On the Fillmore hill between Broadway and Green a curious cable counterbalanced electric line operated from 1896 until 1941. The electric cars were hooked onto a cable, one at the top of the hill and the other at the bottom. The weight of one car going down pulled the second car up. At the end of the haul, the cars would be detached from the cable and continue along their normal routes, powered by the overhead electric wire. (Railway Negative Exchange.)

Powell and Market turntable, 1890s. (Harre Demoro Collection.)

Powell and Market turntable, 1950s.

A Powell Street cable car, 1945.

LEFT.   The Powell-Hyde-Beach Street cable swinging in towards the turntable across the street from the famous Buena Vista Cafe, 1958. The city was yet to landscape the grounds around the turntable and create Victorian Park.

ABOVE.   Hyde Street, late 1950s. (Tom Gray.)

RIGHT.   The car yard behind the Washington-Mason powerhouse. The gripman releases the cable and the car slides backward through the switch and into the yard, 1950s. (Fred Mathews.)

127

California and Powell, late 1950s. (Tom Gray.)

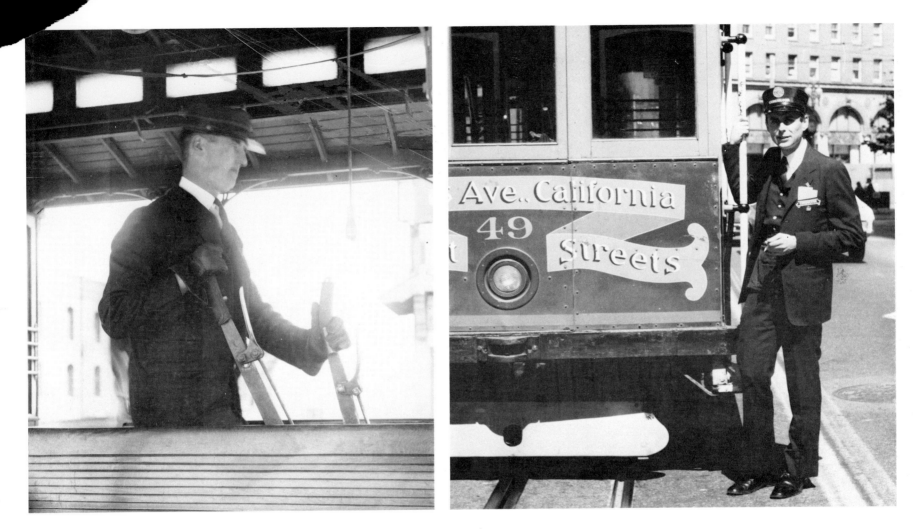

ABOVE.   A California Street Cable Railroad carman, about 1930. In 1934 the Carmen's Union required the company to update their uniforms, the style of which dated back to the earliest days of the cable car.

RIGHT.   Conductor Richard Morley of the California Street line wearing an old-fashioned blue serge uniform, 1980. Muni's regulation uniform now consists of brown pants, a yellow shirt, a brown Eisenhower jacket, and a green beret. (Tom Gray.)

UPPER LEFT.   *Periodically the cable cars get all dressed up. In 1962, the occasion was the 50th birthday of the Municipal Railway. Hotels, banks, department stores, and other businesses sponsored the decorating of the little cars. (Victor Du Brutz.)*

LOWER LEFT & OPPOSITE: *1973—the 100th birthday of the cable cars. Cars were adorned with historic prints and photographs of San Francisco's famous sites and personalities, and with lyrics, spelled out in glittering letters, from the song that has almost become San Francisco's, and the cable cars' anthem: I Left My Heart in San Francisco, "where little cable cars climb halfway to the stars." (Tom Gray.)*

EPILOGUE

The street railway cable car was invented, designed, developed, [per]fected on the hills of San Francisco. Fittingly, the city that gave birth to the picturesque little cars is now the last place on earth where they still operate. And of all the many San Francisco attractions, cable cars are number one. They are colorful and nostalgic, and yet people can actually use them; they are an integral segment of the city's transportation system.

But even so, the future of the slot-tracked railroad has not always been secure, and public agitation has been instrumental in keeping alive the three cable routes that function today.

In 1947, the mayor of San Francisco decreed that the remaining cables be scrapped and replaced by buses. He even declared that he preferred the return to horsecar: "But an almighty rumpus broke out, which finally resulted not in the scrapping of the cars, but in the unseating of the Mayor."

According to Lucius Beebe in his *Cable Car Carnival:*

During the early stages of the battle for the retention of the cables in the face of Mayor Lapham's implacable hostility to the voters, Gump's, the celebrated importers and art shop in Sutter Street and long an integral part of the San Francisco picture, ran a small insertion in *Time* magazine asking for out-of-town reaction to the proposition to scrap the cars. They received thousands of letters, scores of times what the advertising department had expected, from forty states, Hawaii, Alaska, and Canada, all of which, but one solitary communication, cheered for the cables and deplored any form of change whatsoever. The one dissenter was, as San Francisco was delighted to learn, a Los Angeles woman who said the cables disturbed her sleep when in a San Francisco hotel.

Freida Klussman, socialite and civic leader, awakened the populace to the desirability of continuing the cable car heritage. She and her legions were successful in saving the cable cars, but not before part of the system was dismantled, notably the Sacramento-Clay cables. (The city would have been wise to leave that particular steep grade on Clay for even now the diesel buses have to stop occasionally and ask their passengers to walk to the top while the empty bus struggles to make the hill.)

In 1955, lest future mayors might attempt some similar move, a proviso was written into the city charter guaranteeing perpetuation and maintenance of the three surviving lines. No change in this situation may be made with-

Frieda Klussman, defender and champion of the cable cars, receiving a testimonial letter from grateful California Street Cable Railroad employees, 1948.

The "Cable Car Lady's" cable car. 1973. (Tom Gray.)

SAN FRANCISCO CABLE CAR

U.S. 8c

HISTORIC PRESERVATION

Postage stamp issued in 1971.

out a decision by a majority of San Francisco voters. A further nationwide approval was placed on the cable cars in 1964, when the lines were formally designated a National Historic Landmark. A bronze tablet at the Hyde Street turntable notes the site as having "exceptional value in commemorating and illustrating the history of the United States."

Today, even though the cables are still maligned by some as archaic and nonfunctional, the city is preparing to spend millions of dollars to restore and rebuild the system, but this time—perhaps, having learned a lesson on the Clay Street grade—keeping to the original design.

Several years ago, a new car No. 1 was built. Since no plans were available, a group of dedicated people gathered old photographs, measured old cars, and drew up a "new" set of plans for reconstructing the original. The result was so successful that there are now plans to build more new cars during the rebuilding of the cable lines.

The #1 car in 1973. (Tom Gray.)

In 1974, when Hallidie Plaza was built at the entrance of the BART Powell Street station, Powell, between the turntable and Ellis Street, was paved with brick to create a mall and closed to all traffic but cable cars. (Stephen W. Fotter.)

Victorian Park turntable. (Tom Gray.)

California Street cable atop Nob Hill, the Mark Hopkins Hotel in the background. (Tom Gray.)

APPENDIX

Cable Car Lines in Other American Cities

BALTIMORE, MARYLAND

Baltimore Traction Company
Dates: 1891-1896
Mileage: 7.1
Gauge: 5'-4½"
Type of Grip: Side

Baltimore City Passenger Railway
Dates: 1893-1899
Mileage: 10.7
Gauge: 5'-4½"
Type of Grip: Side

BINGHAMTON, NEW YORK

Washington Street & State Asylum R.R.
Dates: 1885-1888
Mileage: .75
Type of Grip: Fairchild twin cable system
Steepest Grade: 10%

BROOKLYN, NEW YORK

Brooklyn Cable Company
Dates: 1887
Mileage: .50
Gauge: 4'-8½"
Type of Grip: Johnson ladder-cable grip

Brooklyn Heights Railroad
Dates: 1891-1909
Mileage: 1.04
Gauge: 4'8½"
Type of Grip: Wheel operated side grip

BUTTE, MONTANA

Butte City Street Railroad
Dates: 1889-1897
Mileage: 1.12
Gauge: 4'-8½"
Type of Grip: Bottom grip
Steepest Grade: 13.2%

CHICAGO, ILLINOIS

Chicago City Railway
Dates: 1882-1906
Mileage: 15.11
Gauge: 4'-8½"
Type of Grip: Double jaw side grip
    No appreciable grade

North Chicago Street Railroad
Dates: 1888-1906
Mileage: 8.6
Gauge: 4'-8½"
Type of Grip: Low & Grim top grip
    No appreciable grade

West Chicago Street Railroad
Dates: 1890-1906
Mileage: 15.2
Gauge: 4'-8½"
Type of Grip: Side grip and bottom grip
    No appreciable grade

CINCINNATI, OHIO

Mount Adams & Eden Park Railway
Dates: 1885-1898
Mileage: 3.8
Gauge: 5'-2½"
Type of Grip: Side

Vine Street Cable Railway
Dates: 1888-1898
Mileage: 4.05
Gauge: 5'-2½"
Type of Grip: Side
Steepest Grade: 8.5%

Mount Auburn Cable Railway
Dates: 1888-1902
Mileage: 4.5
Gauge: 5'-2"
Type of Grip: Bottom
Steepest Grade: 8%

North Chicago Street Railroad. (Railway Negative Exchange.)

Cleveland City Cable Railway.

Denver Tramway Company, 1893. (Denver Regional Transportation District Archives.)

CLEVELAND, OHIO

Cleveland City Cable Railway
Dates: 1890-1901
Mileage: 9.2
Gauge: 4'-8½"
Type of Grip: Side

DENVER, COLORADO

Denver Tramway Company
Dates: 1888-1893
Mileage: 9.3
Gauge: 3'-6'
Type of Grip: Side

Denver City Cable Railway
Dates: 1889-1900
Mileage: 15.00
Gauge: 3'-6"
Type of Grip: Side

GRAND RAPIDS, MICHIGAN

Valley City Street & Cable Rwy.
Dates: 1888-1891
Mileage: 6.9
Gauge: 4'-8½"
Type of Grip: Side

HOBOKEN, NEW JERSEY

North Hudson County Railway
Dates: 1886-1892
Mileage: 1.25
Gauge: 4'8½"
Type of Grip: Bottom
Steepest Grade: 5%

KANSAS CITY, MISSOURI

Kansas City Cable Railway
Dates: 1885-1906
Mileage: 10.00
Gauge: 4'-8½"
Type of Grip: Side
Steepest Grade: 18.54%

Metropolitan Street Railway
Dates: 1887-1913
Mileage: 13.3
Gauge: 4'-8½"
Type of Grip: Side
Steepest Grade: 20%

Grand Avenue Railway
Dates: 1887-1903
Mileage: 8.9
Gauge: 4'-8½"
Type of Grip: Side

Inter-State Consolidated Rapid Transit Company
Dates: 1888-1892
Mileage: 2.53
Gauge: 4'-8½"
Type of Grip: Side
Steepest Grade: 8.8½ (?)

Peoples Cable Railway
Dates: 1888-1899
Mileage: 3.5
Gauge: 4'-8½"
Type of Grip: Side

Union Cable Railway
Dates: 1889
Mileage: 1.51
Gauge: 4'-8½"
Type of Grip: Bottom
Steepest Grade: 11.7%
  This line, beset with technical difficulties, lasted only one day.

LOS ANGELES, CALIFORNIA

Second Street Cable Railroad
Dates: 1885-1890
Mileage: 1.12
Gauge: 3'-6"
Type of Grip: Single jaw side
Steepest Grade: 27.7%

A Los Angeles cable train at Evergreen Cemetery. (The Bancroft Library.)

Philadelphia, Pennsylvania, 1885. (Railway Negative Exchange.)

ABOVE.   *Omaha, Nebraska (Bostwick-Frohardt Collection, KMTV, Omaha.)*

OPPOSITE.   *Consolidated Cable Company. Oakland. (Louis Stein.)*

Temple Street Cable Railway
Dates: 1886-1902
Mileage: 3.5
Gauge: 3'-6"
Type of Grip: Double jaw side
   No major grades

Pacific Railway
Dates: 1889-1895
Mileage: 10.5
Gauge: 3'-6"
Type of Grip: Eppelsheimer bottom
   No major grades

NEWARK, NEW JERSEY
Essex Passenger Railway
Dates: 1888-1889
Mileage: 2.00
Gauge: 5'-2¼"
Type of Grip: Rasmussen non-grip
   system
   This line was completely built, but it is believed that it never carried passengers in revenue service.

NEW YORK, NEW YORK
Third Avenue Railroad
Dates: 1885-1889
Mileage: 14.00
Gauge: 4'-8½"
Type of Grip: Side
   No grades.

Metropolitan Street Railway
Dates: 1893-1901
Mileage: 21.00
Gauge: 4'-8½"
Type of Grip: Side
Steepest Grade: 13.5%

New York & Brooklyn Bridge Rwy.
Dates: 1883-1908
Mileage: 1.00
Gauge: 4'-8½"
Type of Grip: Bottom
   No grades.

OAKLAND, CALIFORNIA
Oakland Cable Railway
Dates: 1886-1899
Mileage: 2.4
Gauge: 3'-6"
Type of Grip: Root side
   No grades. Ran from the current location of Jack London Square, up Broadway and San Pablo Avenue to what is now Emeryville. Built by Senator James G. Fair.

Consolidated Cable Co.
Dates: 1890-1896
Mileage: 5.8
Gauge: 3'-6"
Type of Grip: McClelle bottom grip
Steepest Grade: 14.5
   Although this company was not successful as a cable car railroad, it was the foundation of Borax Smith's transportation empire—the commuter and local transit company known as the Key System. It branched at Broadway and 24th Street, one line going out to Mountain View Cemetery, the other up Oakland Avenue to what is now Highland Avenue in Piedmont. As a very young man, Jack London worked as a coal shoveler in the powerhouse.

OMAHA, NEBRASKA
Cable Tramway Co. of Omaha
Dates: 1887-1895
Mileage: 4.00
Gauge: 4'-8½"
Type of Grip: Side

PHILADELPHIA, PENNSYLVANIA
Philadelphia Traction Co.
Dates: 1885-1895
Mileage: 10.00
Gauge: 5'-2½"
Type of Grip: Top
Steepest Grade: 10% (?)

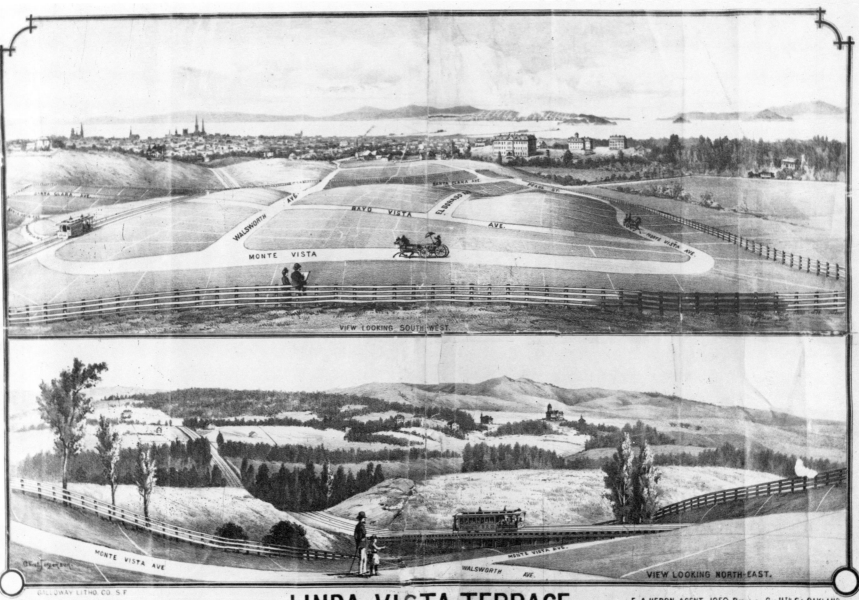

VIEW LOOKING SOUTH WEST.

VIEW LOOKING NORTH-EAST.

LINDA VISTA TERRACE

E. A. HERON, AGENT, 1050 Broadway Cor 11th St. OAKLAND.

GALLOWAY LITHO. CO. S.F.

SITUATED MIDWAY BETWEEN THE CITY HALL AND PIEDMONT, TRAVERSED BY THE LINE OF THE NEW **PIEDMONT CABLE RAILWAY,** A BROAD PLATEAU 186 FEET ABOVE THE BAY HAVING JUST ENOUGH SLOPE TO PRESENT AN **UNOBSTRUCTED PANORAMA** EXTENDING TO THE GOLDEN GATE, ITS COMMANDING POSITION WARRANTS ITS NAME **BEAUTIFUL VIEW**

143

This unique combination cable-electric car was operated by
the Portland (Oregon) Cable Railway in the 1890s. On level
portions of its route it ran as an electric trolley car, but on
hills a grip was installed and the car ran by cable traction.

PITTSBURGH, PENNSYLVANIA

Pittsburgh Traction Company
Dates: 1888-1896
Mileage: 5.4
Gauge: 5'-2½"
Type of Grip: Writton top

Citizens Traction Company
Dates: 1889-1897
Mileage: 5.9
Gauge: 5'-2½"
Type of Grip: Whitton top
Steepest Grade: 5%

Central Traction Company
Dates: 1890-1896
Mileage: 2.9
Gauge: 5'-2½"
Type of Grip: Side
Steepest Grade: 11.1%

PORTLAND, OREGON

Portland Cable Railway
Dates: 1890-1904
Mileage: 3.7
Gauge: 3'-6"
Type of Grip: Bottom
Steepest Grade: 20.93%

PROVIDENCE, RHODE ISLAND

Providence Cable Tramway
Dates: 1889-1895
Mileage: 3.43
Gauge: 4'-8½"
Type of Grip: Side
Steepest Grade: 15%

ST. LOUIS, MISSOURI

St. Louis Cable & Western Rwy.
Dates: 1886-1891
Mileage: 3.2
Gauge: 4'-10"
Type of Grip: Side

Citizens Railway
Dates: 1887-1894
Mileage: 9.65
Gauge: 4'-10"
Type of Grip: Side

Missouri Railroad
Dates: 1881-1901
Mileage: 4.53
Gauge: 4'-10"
Type of Grip: Side

Peoples Railway
Dates: 1890-1901
Mileage: 5.15
Gauge: 4'-10"
Type of Grip: Side

St. Louis Railroad
Dates: 1890-1900
Mileage: 7.57
Gauge: 4'-10"
Type of Grip: Bottom grip

ST. PAUL, MINNESOTA

St. Paul City Railway
Dates: 1888-1898
Mileage: 2.3
Gauge: 4'-8½"
Type of Grip: Side
Steepest Grade: 16%

SAN DIEGO, CALIFORNIA

San Diego Cable Railway
Dates: 1890-1892
Mileage: 4.7
Gauge: 3'-6"
Type of Grip: Van Vleck bottom
Steepest Grade: 8%

Pittsburgh, Pennsylvania. (Railway Negative Exchange.)

St. Louis, Missouri. (Railway Negative Exchange.)

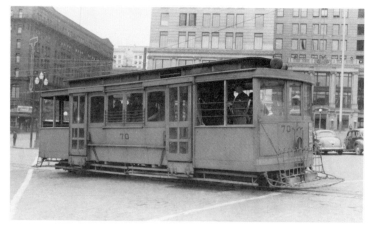

Seattle, Washington, 1938. (Bert Ward.)

Tacoma, Washington, 1930s. (The Bancroft Library.)

SEATTLE, WASHINGTON

Seattle City Railway
Dates: 1888-1940
Mileage: 2.5
Gauge: 3'-6"
Type of Grip: Side
Steepest Grade: 18%

Front Street Cable Railway
Dates: 1889-1900
Mileage: 2.7
Gauge: 4'-8½"
Type of Grip: Side

Madison Street Cable Railway
Dates: 1891-1940
Mileage: 3.6
Gauge: 3'-6"
Type of Grip: Side
Steepest Grade: 20.88%

West Seattle Cable Railway
Dates: 1890-1897
Mileage: 2.0
Gauge: 3'-6"
Type of Grip: ???
Steepest Grade: 16%

Union Trunk Line
Dates: 1891-1940
Mileage: .75
Gauge: 3'-6"
Type of Grip: Side
Steepest Grade: 18.65%

SIOUX CITY, IOWA

Sioux City Cable Railway
Dates: 1889-1894
Mileage: 7.0
Gauge: 4'-8½"
Type of Grip: Side
Steepest Grade: 10.9%

SPOKANE, WASHINGTON

Spokane Cable Railway
Dates: 1889-1894
Mileage: 4.25
Gauge: 3'-0"
Type of Grip: Root side
Steepest Grade: 14.29%

TACOMA, WASHINGTON

Tacoma Railway & Motor Co.
Dates: 1891-1938
Mileage: 1.6
Gauge: 3'-6"
Type of Grip: Root side
Steepest Grade: 14.29%

WASHINGTON, D.C.

Washington & Georgetown R.R.
Dates: 1890-1898
Mileage: 7.9
Gauge: 4'-8½"
Type of Grip: Side

Columbia Railway
Dates: 1895-1899
Mileage: 2.8
Gauge: 4'-8½"
Type of Grip: Side
  This was the last new cable system constructed in the United States.

Seattle, Washington.

Melbourne, Australia.

Projected Lines

Several major American cities proposed cable lines in the 1890s, and many franchises for cable roads were granted. However, the rapid development of the electric streetcar doomed these projects. Actual construction of many roads had been begun, but converted to electric traction use before the laying of cable, notably in Dallas and Minneapolis. In 1888, the West End Street Railway of Boston scrapped all plans for an extensive cable system in favor of converting their horsecar lines to electric traction. It was said that this decision by this great street railway, one of the largest in the world, gave impetus to the decline of cable traction.

Summary of Foreign Installations

Birmingham, England.
1888-1911. 3 miles.

Douglas, Isle of Man.
1896-1929. 1.62 miles.

Dunedin, New Zealand.
1881-1957. 4.97 miles.

Edinburgh, Scotland.
1888-1923. 25.8 miles.

Glasgow, Scotland.
1897-1935. 6.6 miles.
This was the only cable-operated subway.

Lisbon, Portugal.
1890-1912. 2.25 miles.

London, England.
1884-1909. 4.21 miles.

Matlock, England.
1893-1927. 0.62 miles.

Melbourne, Australia.
1885-1940. 1.5 miles.

Paris, France.
1891-1924. 1.5 miles.

Sydney, Australia.
1886-1905. 4.75 miles.

The city of Melbourne used cable cars on many principal transit routes until 1940, even though no hilly terrain indicated their use there as it did in San Francisco, Seattle, and Tacoma. The evolution of city transit systems over the years called for cable lines to be replaced by electric streetcars, which in turn were superceded by motor buses. The Melbourne cable lines were replaced by motor bus in 1940, but a few years later electric streetcars supplanted the bus, a unique reversal.

BIBLIOGRAPHY

Arnold, B.J., *Transportation Facilities of San Francisco*. San Francisco, 1913.

Beebe, Lucius, and Clegg, Charles, *Cable Car Carnival*. Oakland, 1951.

Bolton, Herbert Eugene, trans. and ed., *The San Francisco Colony*. Berkeley, 1930.

The Cable Railway Company's System of Traction Railways for Cities and Towns. San Francisco, 1881. (Original prospectus located in the Special Collections Department of the San Francisco Public Library and reprinted by the Public Service Office of the Mayor for the Centennial of the Cable Car, 1973.)

Hilton, George W., *The Cable Car in America*, Howell-North, Berkeley, 1971.

Inside Track, house organ of The Market Street Railway Company, San Francisco, 1922-1938.

Kahn, Edgar, *Cable Car Days in San Francisco*. Stanford, 1945.

Moulin, Tom, and DeNevi, Don, *San Francisco: Creation of a City*. Celestial Arts, Millbrae, California, 1978.

Parker, Frank, *Anatomy of the San Francisco Cable Car*. James Ladd Delkin, Stanford, 1946.

Smallwood, Charles, *The White Front Cars of San Francisco*. Interurbans, Glendale, California, 1978.

Street Railway Journal. Street Railway Publishing Co., New York, 1891-1896.

Watkins, T.H., and Olmsted, R.R., *Mirror of the Dream*, Scrimshaw Press, San Francisco, 1976.

Roy Graves San Francisco Collection, Bancroft Library, University of California, Berkeley.

San Francisco Public Utilities Commission, various reports.

San Francisco newspapers and periodicals, various back issues.

Company reports and record books of Market Street Cable Railway Company (1890-1902), United Railroads of San Francisco (1902-1921), and Market Street Railway (1921-1942) from the collection of the late Charles D. Miller and kindly made available to the authors by Mrs. Julia Miller.

INDEX